From

Full House

To

Empty Nest

BOX 3566 · GRAND RAPIDS, MI 49501

PUBLISHING BOOKS THAT FEED
THE SOUL WITH THE WORD OF GOD.

From
Full House
To
Empty Nest

William L. Coleman

From Full House To Empty Nest
Copyright © 1994 by William L. Coleman

Discovery House Publishers is affiliated with Radio Bible Class, Grand Rapids, Michigan

Discovery House books are distributed to the trade by Thomas Nelson Publishers, Nashville, Tennessee 37214

Library of Congress Cataloging-in-Publication Data

Coleman, William L.
    From full house to empty nest / William L. Coleman.
       p.   cm.
    ISBN 0-929239-82-2
    1. Empty nesters—United States—Life skills guides. 2. Parent and adult child—United States. I. Title.
    HQ1063.6.C66 1994
    306.874—dc20   94-33944
                                         CIP

Printed in the United States of America

94 95 96 97 98 / CHG / 10 9 8 7 6 5 4 3 2 1

Contents

Thanks for the help!

Many groups and individuals shared freely of their time and experience to make this book possible. I am most grateful for their willingness to talk about this subject. In particular I want to thank some special friends for coming together and letting me pick their brains:

Menno and Susanna Classen
Dale and Jean Jackson
Rich and Lois Janzen
Don and Joyce Kupfersmith
Gary and Sandy Samuelson

The good work, encouragement, and help given by the staff at Discovery House should be noted. An extra salute for the fine support of Bob DeVries and Carol Holquist. Their labors went a long way to make this book a reality.

Naturally, I have changed the stories, shuffling some and scrunching others. The illustrations are true but have been rearranged to protect the storytellers.

A New Way of Flying

These don't have to be fearful, lonely years. Many "graduate" parents are finding this to be a happy, rewarding time after the children leave home.

But in order for this to happen, some adjustments need to be made. Smart people take the time to read, listen, and learn how to make those changes as smoothly as possible. This book is written to help the reader close up the nest, not for the winter, but forever, and begin a new way of flying.

My wife Pat and I have been there. We have experienced the joy, the nostalgia, the heartache, and the happiness. It isn't easy to test our older wings, but it must be done. All of us need to leap off the branch and soar into the air for ourselves again.

Expect a few downdrafts. Don't be surprised if you get nervous. Sometimes you may even wish you could go back and gather the chicks under your wings again. But relax a little and that feeling should go away.

For most of us these are great years. Spread your wings and see what new ways God wants you to fly.

"They will soar on wings like eagles" (Isaiah 40:31).

The Smells and Sounds of Parenting

I know exactly how you feel. For twenty-five years I was a practicing parent. Like you, I have had suckers stuck to my trousers, wet gumballs put in my pockets, and my best tie used as a kite tail.

I know what it's like to be thrown up on. You get dressed up, ready to go out for the evening. You tell yourself not to pick up the baby that last time, but you do it anyway. As soon as your princess rests on your shoulder, you hear that unmistakable gurgling noise, and there it goes. The baby vomits generously all over your best clothes.

Strained apricots. Regurgitated strained apricots. You try to wipe them off but it's too late. All evening you are going to smell like apricots.

Every parent knows what that is like. We don't talk about it. There are a lot of things we can't bring ourselves to talk about, but they are there.

Ever eaten the rest of a hamburger that's been slobbered on? Admit it. You'll feel better. You can still taste that warm wetness in your mouth, can't you?

Young couples without children can't appreciate this. They've only read about it or seen it on video. Parents our age have lived through it.

If you're a parent, I know how you drive a car. You drive it with only your left hand on the steering wheel. That's so you can reach back and "correct" the kids with your right. You have to stop little Kevin from feeding crayons to Susie and keep Taylor from latching the dog's flea collar too tight.

Watch when parents walk into a room. You can always tell. The right arm is longer than the left. That comes from driving with kids in the car.

If you're a parent, you've probably gone camping. Nine families out of ten go camping. There are two reasons for that. One, it's good for the family; and two, it's cheap.

We took our children camping in a tent when all three were preschoolers. The babies were still in diapers. And when I say diapers I don't mean the new ones—the Huggies or Snuggies or Buggies or whatever. We had real diapers. The kind you kept like trophies.

When we broke camp we placed a pail of water on the floor behind the front seat. One by one we dumped the diapers into the bucket. Then we all climbed into the car, rolled down the windows and drove across Ohio in 104-degree heat.

At the next campsite we all stumbled out of the car barely able to breathe. We hugged the trees. We kissed the bushes. We learned to love the great outdoors. Those were the good days.

You never rid smells like that from your nose. Once a parent, always a parent.

Children are a blessing

Most of us prayed for children. We prayed before we got them and we prayed much harder after they arrived. Maybe that's one of the reasons why God gave them to us—so we would talk to Him more. It worked.

We actually wanted children. They weren't a nuisance. We didn't consider them roadblocks interfering with our trip to success. When the doctor said we were going to have another addition to the family, we didn't sit down and discuss our options.

That was happy news and we smiled from ear to ear. If we cried, it was for joy. We wanted to be a family and if possible a family meant children.

> Sons are a heritage from the LORD,
> children a reward from him.
> Like arrows in the hands of a warrior
> are sons born in one's youth.
> Blessed is the man
> whose quiver is full of them (Psalm 127:3–5a).

It was a simpler day. We had fewer choices to make, but we weren't looking for choices. We knew a good thing when we heard it. God was giving us a child. We felt like God had placed His hand on us and given us the grand prize.

We felt like Samuel's mother, Hannah. When she heard God was going to make her a mother she began to pray so enthusiastically that people thought she was drunk.

When our baby was finally born, I remember paying the hospital bill with the cash we had saved during those nine months. It was a simpler day.

A nervous blessing

We accepted our children as divine gifts. The gifts seemed terribly fragile and unpredictable. We carried them around like giant cream puffs, afraid we would drop them or bump them against the wall.

How many parents have put a finger under their baby's tiny nostrils to make sure they were still breathing? How many have been afraid their infant was deaf? At some time most parents sneak up behind their baby and slam a book to see if he can hear. The poor infant jumps a foot off the bed, eyes leaping out like springs, startled, and screaming. But Mom and Dad are so pleased to discover that the one-month-old can hear.

Parents pay their dues. They walk the floor at night with a child who can't stop crying and coughing. They wonder whether to call the doctor, rush to the hospital, or try once more to rock him to sleep. Parents care and love and do what it takes to nurture their children while they are in the womb and far beyond.

Do you remember your first shock when you learned it is twenty-four-hour care? The child doesn't go back to the hospital at night to be returned at 9:00 a.m. When the baby wants to eat, it sets off a dinner siren that won't quit and can't be ignored until its needs are met.

This was only the beginning. Their needs changed, their mobility increased, and many of their predicaments became more harrowing. They were always fragile to their parents, even when they became thirty years old and had children of their own.

"Every good and perfect gift is from above, coming down from the Father of the heavenly lights, who does not change like shifting shadows" (James 1:17).

They grew up

With mixed emotions we watched the children grow from age to age and stage to stage. Most parents seem to prefer some stages over others. Preschoolers, grade school, puberty, and high school each have their own distractions. Some parents hate the teething days while others dread the teen years.

The ages we feared the most were often the same stages which were difficult as we grew up. If we drove our parents nuts while we were in junior high school, we were probably distrustful of our own early teenagers. Many mothers found their own fourth- and fifth-grade days ideal. They had been excellent students and the complications of adolescence had not yet hit them. Consequently they loved relating to their own fourth- and fifth-graders. Because they didn't expect trouble at that age, conflicts were less likely to happen.

Other parents are little more than overgrown teenagers themselves. As suspended adolescents, they live for the day when they can share with teenagers on the same level.

In some ways raising children is like race car driving. The acceleration and adrenaline are often terrific. It is a challenge to be part of their lives and watch them take each new bend in the road. At the same time the tension of it all begins to show. The fun is waiting up late to see them come home after the big event. Likewise the pain is waiting up late to see them come home from the big event.

That's the way it should be. Raising children is by and large a great experience. But how many of us would like to do it a second time? Not many hands go up. Not many volunteer to go through a second twenty-five years or so.

We've all been there. We've sat in recitals and listened as our children took their turns playing some clanging tune. We've sweat blood hoping they would hit the right keys, keep their dress down, and not pick their nose.

Can you remember when she qualified for the regional spelling contest? That meant you drove her and three of her giggling friends halfway across the state to be ready at 9:00 a.m. Do you remember twisting your hands while she spelled "serendipity" and you felt so proud that your child was so bright?

Can you also remember hoping her 4–H singing group would lose so you wouldn't have to take next Thursday off and drive her to the state capitol to compete again? Then you felt guilty for hoping that your own daughter would lose.

As they grew you remembered Shakespeare's remark about all the world being a stage. You watched each act as your children performed, took their bows, and moved to the next stage.

And then the day came. They packed their clothes, took the posters off the walls and moved toward the door. The big transition had arrived. They were actually moving out.

One by one they left

If you have done it, you never forget. You stand in your driveway and wave goodbye as your adult child leaves home. In your eye a tear builds and finally trickles down your cheek. But what no one can hear is the chuckle in the back of your throat.

We really hurt to see them leave. And we are really glad to see them go.

Twenty years of joy and happiness and grief and tension. Twenty years of wondering where they were and what they were up to. Two decades of pride and satisfaction. Two decades of broken things. At first broken dishes and knickknacks. Then broken windows and mirrors. And broken bones. Recently broken cars with dented bumpers and smashed headlights.

And sometimes broken hearts. Broken with gladness when they went on their first date. Broken with sadness the first time you realized they had lied to you.

They leave. Soon other friends will take your place. Their friends will become closer and more intimate. At first your children will call you just to talk or to ask advice. Too soon the calls will taper off as they find new people who will also listen.

"For this reason a man will leave his father and mother and be united to his wife, and they will become one flesh" (Genesis 2:24).

We remember accompanying our first daughter, Mary, as she left for college. The University of Nebraska is a quiet campus compared to many. We borrowed a pickup truck and moved her stuff to the eighth floor at Abel dormitory.

As we finished unloading, we looked hard at the atmosphere surrounding her. Young men were tossing food out of the twelfth-story windows to the pavement below. A campus policeman attempted to write a ticket for double-parking while students shouted obscenities at him. Across the street a platform was being constructed for a rock concert.

We each hugged Mary, bade her a fond farewell, ran for our car, and locked ourselves in. Sadly, we headed west for the safety of our home.

The family was beginning to separate and we were starting our new lives.

Biblical principles for separating

The family has a natural progress. We grow up, leave home, and start a family of our own. There are exceptions, but most of us still do it like this. It's the way God put the family in motion.

As we watch our children leave, we can find strength in several biblical guidelines that will help us move into the next stage. These principles will assure us that everything is normal and blessed by God.

1. *Thank God for your arrows* (Psalm 127:3–5).

Children always have been a great idea. Most of them have enriched our lives. If we fail to see them as gifts from God, it is easy to become bitter and lonely. God has been good, even when the children have chosen to wander astray.

If we lose our sense of gratitude we will lose sight of God's terrific handiwork.

2. *Leave and cleave is a step up* (Ephesians 5:31).

When our children leave home and start their own families, we have gained something wonderful. If we see that as a loss, our concept of family is twisted.

Grown children are like ships; they need to be launched. Some can't leave. Quite a few return. But never grieve over the ones who sail on with their own families.

3. *Be willing to let go* (Luke 15, prodigal son).

Even when our children are not the polished trophies we had hoped they would be, we need to let go. The father of the prodigal must have been extremely apprehensive to see his self-centered son leave. But it had to happen.

Children are like tomatoes; once they start to ripen, they need to be picked. Otherwise they erupt and lose their flavor. Timing is everything. When it's time, it's time.

4. *Become a golden apple* (Proverbs 17:6).

The time is soon coming when the grown children will look up to their parents and be proud of them. The volcanic years of adolescence have passed and a lake of peace is forming in the cove. Teenagers who used to be embarrassed at the sight of their parents have become young adults who admire their gray-haired, middle-aged relatives.

We start to collect a little dignity.

5. *The blessings will start coming again.*

In Proverbs 31:28 the Bible says, "Her children arise and call her blessed." They don't usually do that right away. It takes a little maturity before grown children will tell their parents "Thank you." But it happens. Every day you will become a little smarter, a little wiser, a tad more sensible in the eyes of your children; and they might even start telling you so.

6. *Get ready for the grandkids* (Psalm 128:6).

"And may you live to see your children's children." Life doesn't depend on grandchildren, but they certainly add spunk to aching bones. I notice that my friends have become silly, proud, doting, and giddy. They are having more fun than people on blood-pressure pills should be allowed to have.

Most graduate parents I know seem to be surviving very well. Their grins are wider. Their eyes sparkle a little brighter. They have more spring in their steps. And almost all the ones I meet are going someplace. They are hurrying off to golf, to pick strawberries, to get the grandkids, to take part in some ministry.

God seems to have given us extra bounce. After all, there's a lot we need to get at and see to.

The Major Shift

Remember the events that used to fill our lives? Piano lessons, plays, concerts, Little League, birthday parties, church programs, field trips, art contests, spelling bees, 4–H projects, and Camp Hugo Hunka. Did you ever have a green, slimy science project in your refrigerator right next to the tapioca pudding? Were you ever up late at night typing your child's social studies paper?

If you recognize most of that, you can remember what kind of activities filled your life. They weren't always the things we chose to do, though they sometimes were. Just as often they were what we were obligated to get involved in.

And now it has changed. Ask your friends these questions:

- How long has it been since you went to a piano recital?
- Do you still attend Friday night school games?
- Do you still stay up until 1:00 a.m. listening for the front door to open?

- When was the last time you picked up four children for a birthday party?

Unless you are well into your grandparenting years, most of these activities are turning into snapshots from the past. Since many of us centered our lives on parenting, we are now left with sizable gaps in our time schedules. It was as if our children's needs dictated how we spent our energies.

We can now expect to make serious adjustments as we come down from our high of raising children. If you drive a car all day through the hills of West Virginia, what will happen when you try to sleep that night? Most likely you will work the brakes and maneuver the steering wheel as you toss and turn in bed.

The same is true of parenting. It's hard to simply park the car and turn off the engine. And if you do, you will still change diapers, fix lunches, push swings, and tell children to clean up their rooms in your sleep.

Round-the-clock mothering

Parents who have the most trouble making the shift are the ones who mothered or fathered constantly. Those who allowed themselves the luxury of other interests can slide more smoothly into the next stage of life.

For instance, parents who cared for a severely handicapped child usually have trouble making the transition. These conscientious and sacrificing parents have been involved in twenty-four-hour care for as long as a decade or two. They slept with one eye open and one ear tuned. Their child's needs called for all of their attention and energy. When that situation changes, the parent may have a difficult time moving into a different schedule.

The same can be said of parents who had little or no interests other than children. If Mom always put her children first, if she worried about them even when she was off bowling, if she constantly called to make sure everything was all right, she was a round-the-clock mother.

Consequently she may have neglected other areas that would have made her a more well-rounded person. She may have let her personal and spiritual development slide; her relationship as a wife may have lagged; her opportunities for exercise and entertainment and culture may have dropped to near zero. This mother majored on sacrifice. Others came first. She was a good and devoted mother who loved her children. Even if she worked outside the home, her first concern was the children.

But now the children don't need her in the same way they once did. She must, through the natural process, withdraw and concentrate on her own life. Many great mothers are ill-equipped to make that move.

It's going to hurt. There could be panic attacks. There could be enormous anxiety. And, frankly, some mothers and fathers never successfully make the leap from constant care for others to the place where they take on a life of their own.

Naomi withdraws

One of the best examples in the Bible of parental withdrawal is found in the book of Ruth. Naomi had lost her husband, Elimelech, in death; and later both of her sons, Mahlon and Kilion, died. That left Naomi with two daughters-in-law, Orpah and Ruth.

No doubt Naomi felt great affection for the women who had married her sons. But when she heard that there was no longer a famine in her homeland, Naomi decided to return to Judah and make her own life. She was not going to depend on her daughters-in-law.

Some aged and frail relatives are dependent and no one begrudges them that contact. But Naomi could still forge her own way and she was determined to do it.

You have to give Naomi an *A* for grit. It has never been easy to be a widow, and it was even harder in those days. Because their job and work opportunities were extremely limited, they generally relied on their families for support. Naomi had very little immediate family, but she was willing to leave even those to strike out on her own.

The story tells how the three women walked down the road that led from Moab to Judah. Naomi asked God to bless her daughters-in-law and asked that the Lord would find them new husbands. Then she kissed each of the women and told them to go back to their people.

As we know, Orpah went back and Ruth refused. She was determined to go wherever her mother-in-law went and even follow Naomi's God.

What a woman Naomi was. Since she could be independent, she chose that freedom for herself and for the people she loved. After living among them for ten years, it was difficult to cut the cord, but she was set on doing it.

Hope lies in the future

The words *hope* and *future* are almost redundant. Hope deals with tomorrows and not yesterdays. Too many of us believe our best hope is to cling to what used to be. We are afraid of losing the past. While that's understandable, it may not be reasonable.

My wife's Aunt Nell is in her eighties and she is continuously planning for tomorrow. She had always wanted to go on a cruise, so recently she did. She just made plans to fly across the country to her great-niece's wedding. Every year on the day after Christmas Nell buys Christmas cards for next year at half-price. This grand lady keeps looking forward and not behind.

The biblical writers encourage us to do exactly that. The question is still the same as when we were eight years old. "What do you want to do when you grow up?" The answer is to put our major efforts into this twenty-four hours.

Keep pressing on.

Never get stuck in yesterday whether it was good or bad. Life is more than a picture album. The present is what we are living in.

"Forgetting what is behind and straining toward what is ahead, I press on toward the goal to win the prize for which God has called me heavenward in Christ Jesus" (Philippians 3:13–14).

Straining toward what is ahead is where the Christian life is. Many veteran parents are bogged down in their regrets about the past. Others keep basking in the delights of yesterday. Unfortunately a few simply quit living when the last child packs her bags. The question should be, "What next?" Paul pressed on toward the goal.

One step at a time.

Certainly it's frightening to take the next step in our lives. Each new stage carries its own price and uncertainty. That's why it helps to trust God as we put each foot forward in our new independence.

When the Israelites stood at the Red Sea, the Lord told Moses, "Tell the Israelites to move on" (Exodus 14:15). With the Egyptian army at their backs and the sea in front, it didn't look like they had a good choice. Any of us might have trembled, hesitated, and waffled with that kind of decision to make.

But the word came, "Move on." Parents have to put their feet in the water, take one step at a time, and begin to experience the next twenty or thirty years.

Hard to withdraw into a vacuum

If someone stops smoking, he might chew gum to take its place. Others eat more and gain weight when they stop smoking. Often the best thing to do is to replace an old habit with a new and constructive habit. If you chew your nails, you may need to find something else to do with your hands.

Let's ask ourselves what we did for our children that we don't do anymore and find a reasonable substitute. Not just any substitute, but a satisfying replacement.

For instance a mother says she constantly cooked meals for her children and she misses it. Cooking for herself or her husband doesn't have nearly the bang it used to have.

Rather than mourn the loss of cooking opportunities, she might ask for whom she could now cook? Make a list:

1. Have people over for evening or weekend meals.
2. Bake for the neighbors and their children.
3. Volunteer at the local mission one day a week.
4. Help cook at camp for one week in the summer.
5. Bake cookies for the grown kids.
6. Mail cookies to unsuspecting friends near and far.
7. Offer to teach cooking for young mothers at the church or in the neighborhood.

The list is limited only by your imagination and energy. Look at what we miss about parenting and see what some of the possible substitutes might be.

What we miss	*Substitutes*
Tending little children.	Nursery, neighbor kids, Headstart, children's church.
Busy evenings.	Take a class, teach a class, have friends over, go to a concert, do couple things.
Having people around.	Call people and invite them over.
Giving presents.	Many children, near and far, would appreciate your generosity.
Taking children places.	Invite children from broken homes to the park, the circus, to play ball.

Interacting with teenagers.	Ask the leader of youth group how you can help.
Sharing your faith.	Befriend a young person who doesn't have a Christian family.
Fixing things.	Fix a kid's bike or electronic equipment.
Reading stories.	Ninety million kids want to be read to.
Miss your grandchildren.	Care about a child; buy him an ice cream cone, push him on a swing, and fuss over him.

It isn't enough to tell an overweight person "Don't eat." For most the shift is painful. But he could eat less and become more active.

We need to look for the big four.

1. *Find someone to love.*

Both God and people (Mark 12:30–31).

2. *Find someone to serve.*

Both God and people (2 Corinthians 4:5).

3. *Set new goals* (Philippians 3:13–14).

4. *Take time for ourselves.*

Enjoy learning and exercise (1 Timothy 4:8).

God has many good ways to work through us in the days to come. It's time to be alert to the new challenges before us.

Breaking a Twenty-Five Year Habit

When Brenda volunteered for the local Headstart program, she was meeting a number of needs. First, she wanted to help a dozen preschoolers, even if it was only a couple of days a month. Second, Brenda knew she had some skills that she wanted to use. Having nurtured children most of her adult life, she missed the interaction, the caring, and the sharing.

Not only is Brenda well qualified to work with children, she has a better disposition than ever. When her four children were living at home she was often tired, harried, and over-extended. Now she is well equipped to show love in short doses to children who need all the extra attention they can get.

Millions of parents have been able to break their dependence on their own children by investing their skills in the lives of others. Too many parents come to a sudden dead stop. Yesterday they had people to care for. Today their children are gone and their lives seem empty.

That's when we are tempted to reach back and hold on to our grown children.

Psychologists say that people who retire with nothing to do tend to die quickly. Many return to the work force in a few years because they feel empty. It's understandable that when parents graduate from parenting they look for other opportunities to nurture.

The call for veteran parents

A few "veteran" mothers got together and decided to put their expertise to work at a public library. During children's story time a dozen young mothers would sit around, holding coats, waiting for their tots and toddlers. The graduate mothers began meeting with the waiting mothers to discuss the fine art of mothering.

From then on the young mothers were as excited about going to story time as their children. Everyone benefited because a few mothers got extra mileage out of their nurturing skills.

There is a biblical principle that tells us this is a smart way to go. It explains that older women have a great deal to offer if they will share their mothering skills.

"They can train the younger women to love their husbands and children" (Titus 2:4).

In the Omaha newspaper an announcement appears regularly describing family night at a local church. The evening consists of exercise for adults plus tutoring for children. It's easy to imagine volunteers helping students with math homework, social studies, and dangling modifiers. Probably many of the tutors are veteran parents between ages forty-five and seventy-five who have too much to offer to quit now.

Some congregations and community centers are particularly blessed because they put Titus 2:4 to work. Mothers teach sewing and cooking, help prepare taxes, and supply baby-sitting, and nurses give immunization shots. A church I was part of started a series of support groups, but immediately the problem arose over who would watch the children. Two fantastic Christian grandmothers volunteered to tend that flock and everyone breathed a sigh of relief. They knew the children were in expert hands.

In the same passage in Titus 2 similar guidelines apply to men. Verses 6 and 7 tell us this: "Similarly, encourage the young men to be self-controlled. In everything set them an example by doing what is good."

Veteran fathers can be seen in Haiti, Brazil, Appalachia, and in hundreds of camps across the nation. They teach knife and gun safety, auto mechanics, carpentry, backpacking, and other skills. They are role models and teach young men how to be good husbands and fathers.

Men who have contributed so much to their own families are now freed up to share with other men of all ages. There is no need for any of us to fade away simply because our children have grown.

Many of us go on for years before we get to be grandparents. Some of us never will be. Others have grandchildren who live a thousand miles away. If it is possible, we invest our nurturing skills in those grandchildren. But for most of us there is plenty of extra energy to go around, and there is no end to the opportunities.

The God of change

Change is hard. It can be rewarding, exciting, ful-filling, and tons of fun, but it is usually difficult. As we redirect our nurturing skills, we are fortunate to have a heavenly Father who is the God of change.

New events, new challenges, new opportunities, new lives are normal with God. The Bible is rich with the word "new" because God is not simply dedicated to the past. It speaks of: • new self •new and living way •new creation • new command • new every morning • new growth • new man • new attitude • new teaching • new song • new birth • new spirit • new covenant.

These are just a few. The word *change* doesn't need to be frightening. But those who run from it will have trouble adapting to an ever-changing family situation.

It's true that God's character doesn't change (Mala-chi 3:6). But God is continuously infusing change into the lives of His people.

Take special note of how God dealt with Saul. He was reluctant to believe that God had chosen him King of Israel and hesitant to follow Samuel, but the Scrip-ture simply says, "God changed Saul's heart" (1 Samuel 10:9).

When we try to hold on to the past and wrap our-selves in the security of yesterday, we may miss the great blessing that God has for us today.

How do we change?

That's the question we have asked parents. As they break out of their parenting role, what new life do they find open to them?

The leading responses we found were these:

1. *We are more relaxed.*

The evidence is overwhelming. Raising children is tough. For all of its benefits, the process is draining, taxing, worrisome, sacrificial, and burdensome. If there are parents who want to claim that it was all a day at the beach, who are we to argue with them? All we know is that most of us considered it hard work. Rewarding hard work, maybe, but real work nevertheless.

Daily tensions have reduced dramatically. We don't worry about homework, meals on varied schedules, clothes, tying up the telephone, what time they will get in, parties, police cars, pregnancy, or shoe styles. Never again will we have to serve paper routes, check out boyfriends, teach anyone to drive, cough up money for school (what a graphic description), or worry how our sense of humor is affecting their psyche.

Even our kids notice the difference and tell us so. It's almost as if they see us as new people. "Whatever happened to uptight Dad?" "Why doesn't Mom have white knuckles anymore?" "Our parents no longer act like detectives."

Reduced anxiety is a major reason why these are the golden years. If our health is decent, we have a new freedom that we haven't known for years.

The temptation is to slip back into uneasiness. We care about our grown children, but some of us still worry.

Many of us have done what this couple does. Their daughter has moved to New York City to pursue a career. In this modern age her parents have cable television, which allows them to watch the New York evening news twice a night. Every time they hear of a young woman who has been mugged, arrested, raped, murdered, or otherwise maltreated, they listen carefully for the details. Was a name given, how old was she, what side of town was this on? They squint their eyes to see the color of the car. If the information is incomplete they call their daughter "just to say hello."

In a city of 18 million people, over a thousand miles away, they still try to track their kid's activities and worry about her safety. But it doesn't have to be that way.

2. *We have more time.*

Free time becomes a real challenge for the middle-aged. Many have gasped for extra time, and now that they have it they aren't sure what to do.

Some veteran parents dive into new pursuits.

Some roll back their eyes and stare at the ceiling.

Some start to pick at their spouses and create trouble.

The new saying could be "Idle hands are the divorce lawyer's tools." A sudden influx of countless, empty hours is difficult for most of us to handle. The time adjustment is too much for many to cope with.

A gift of time can be a good investment in other things that count in life. We can use it to travel, to learn new hobbies, to renew our romance, to find ways to serve Christ, and minister to others. We can widen our horizons. Satisfied people don't let time fritter away or allow extra time to become destructive. Quality time is time with a purpose.

3. *We have more money.*

Most graduate parents may not be rich, but the majority of them have more discretionary income. That's

why you can get into the movies at a discount rate starting at age fifty-five. And you thought it was because the
cinemas felt sorry for you! Not at all. They know you
have money, and they want it. The manager hopes you
go to six movies a week.

If you have a little more cash, thank God for it and
use it well. You can remember only too vividly the days
when you couldn't afford the $80 tennis shoes your child
simply had to have.

More money translates into more opportunity.
Where do you want to go, whom do you want to help,
what do you want to accomplish? Many parents are able
to help their third or fourth child through college more
than they could the first child. Don't feel guilty. Situations change. Be smart, be wise, be adaptable.

One warning flare goes up. With a little extra cash it
could be tempting to meddle in an adult child's life. A couple of hundred here, a couple of hundred there, a thousand
on a special occasion. It's okay to be kind, but always ask
if there is an underlying motive to these fits of generosity.

4. *We eat out more.*

I can remember our elementary-age children talking
about going out to eat. One child said to the other, "Maybe we can talk Mom and Dad into taking us out to someplace special for Christmas."

"Who are you kidding?" the other replied. "They
only took us to McDonald's on Easter."

Many families seldom went out to eat. Too many
children. Too expensive. Sometimes too much trouble.
But now that the children are gone, parents seem to
bounce from restaurant to restaurant.

There are several reasons for those culinary adventures.

- They can afford it.
- It's less fun cooking for two.
- They don't like eating at home staring at the wall or at each other.
- They know of restaurants and foods they would like to try.
- It's part of the good life and they are able to enjoy it.

5. *We travel more.*

Whether it is daylong rides, weekend jaunts, cruises, or mission trips, there is a great increase in mobility—partly because we want to see the world, partly because we want to help others, and also because we are restless. Untethered from some of the responsibilities we have known, these trips are frequently among the best times of our lives.

If our health is still fairly good (and for many that is true), we find our new life extremely fulfilling. Those who remain trapped in the illusion of parenting are the ones who suffer from unnecessary burdens.

Being Weaned from Our Children

There was a time when our children needed us daily. Without us they would have eaten dog food, left the goldfish on the table and put fruit tarts in the VCR. That's the truth. If we hadn't protected them, our children might have grown up to sing in a rock band, gotten a tattoo, and married Lenny, the politician's kid.

Who could question how much they depended on us? Now, we are discovering the other side of that coin. As much as they needed their parents, their parents have also grown to need them.

Parenting became a natural function for us, not unlike sneezing, blinking, and caring. Not only did we lie awake waiting for them to come home, now we know that we wanted to be awake. Our children needed to be held, and now we find out that we loved holding our children.

They held our heart strings in their hands and played us like violins. Now that they have left home, our hearts are lonely and entirely too quiet. We long to hear our children play another tune on our mellow souls.

Do you find it hard?

Don't be too quick to shrug off this question. Losing our children is no piece of cake. Be fair to yourself and take this little test. It will give you some idea of how well you are making the transition.

1. When you don't visit your children or they don't visit you, do you get bored, begin to twitch, and don't know what to do with yourself?

2. Have you discovered that your children are your only hobby?

3. When you do talk to your children, do you have to resist the phrase, "I told you so"?

4. Do you think your son is not being fed properly?

5. Do you ask when more grandchildren are expected?

6. Are you still trying to manipulate your grown child's education?

7. Do you use money to feel needed?

8. Are most of your plans "tentative" in case "the children need me"?

9. Are you unwilling to let your children make the same mistakes you made at their age?

10. Are your children your only friends?

11. Do you have trouble using your daughter's former bedroom as a den even though she is thirty-four years old?

12. Do you drop hints that your child has gained a lot of weight?

How are you doing so far? There are plenty of other questions. Some may be unique to you and your situation. This type of introspection is well worth the effort. Otherwise we may not be able to see how much we are holding on.

The second weaning

Mothers manage to wean their children the first time though it is difficult for some. The special bonding between mother and child is not easily disturbed.

After twenty years she is asked to go through a second weaning. Her adult son or daughter is figuratively taken from her bosom. For all of its joy there is a sense of postpartum blues. Life will never be the same again. Both parent and child know that.

The second weaning, like the first, should bring a sense of peace, accomplishment, and satisfaction. Everyone knew this day was coming. They have known it for years. It should have been an occasion for praising God and great appreciation.

It is a passage into adulthood. No one should attempt to block that passage or hinder it in any way. A second weaning could leave the parents just as happy and full of anticipation as it leaves the grown child.

The fear of change

Our great-grandparents probably didn't have the problem of parent-weaning. They had more children and on the average didn't live as long as we live.

Today we have only two or three children and frequently have them out of the home by the time we are fifty. With a longer life expectancy we are looking at an additional thirty years without children at home.

Relatively young, not knowing where to turn, we turn back to our offspring. It's scary out in the world alone without the children. Trying to break the habit cold-turkey is almost more than we can handle. Shaking, uncertain, afraid, we reach out and try to hold on to our escaping children.

That desperate attempt to keep raising our children creates havoc for both generations. This may be one of the reasons why we are eager to help with college funds. Not only is it generous on our part, but it allows us the opportunity to keep parenting for another four to six years.

Given the chance, most of us tend to fight change. Change is uncertain. Change is painful. We try to resist it even when we know that everyone will benefit from the results.

Attachment to something harmful is never beneficial. And yet we hold on to the past like a kitten hanging onto a limb because it is afraid of what will happen if it lets go or jumps.

A large part of our Christian faith consists of giving our fears to God. He gives us hope in the middle of a changing, trying situation.

Biblical guidelines

There may be no easy way to break an old habit. Fortunately God provides several guidelines which will help parents survive their post-postpartum blues. As with most transitions, we need the stability and reassurance which the Scriptures can offer.

1. Commit our grown children to God.

Look at Acts 20:32. When Paul met with fellow believers from Ephesus on his way to Jerusalem, he knew uncertainty awaited him. The parting was tough. The future was cloudy. But tenderly he told the people he loved, "Now I commit you to God and to the word of his grace, which can build you up and give you an inheritance among all those who are sanctified."

What a magnificent blessing Paul bestowed on the people he cared for. Since they couldn't stay together, Paul committed them into the safekeeping of the God he served. Our children are in His hands and not ours.

2. Ask God to watch over them.

It is not that we have washed our hands of them but rather that we have called for a first-class security guard, our heavenly Father. Our children are not orphaned but rather are protected by the ultimate Parent.

We won't be able to watch over them every hour or hide in the attic of their lives. But the Great Watchman will be there. Every time a parent prays for a grown child, he clings to that promise and hope.

> The LORD watches over you—
> the LORD is your shade at your right hand;
> the sun will not harm you by day,
> nor the moon by night.
> The LORD will keep you from all harm—
> he will watch over your life;
> the LORD will watch over your coming and going
> both now and forevermore (Psalm 121:5–8).

Type up these verses and paste them on your bathroom mirror. Every time you think of your children, claim these verses.

3. *Put your confidence and trust in the Lord.*

It's hard to break an old habit because we lack confidence in our ability to handle change. Instead of worrying about our weaknesses, we should place our full trust in God's ability. He will give us strength for the day, even when the separation makes us shaky.

> When I am afraid,
> I will trust in you.
> In God, whose word I praise,
> in God I trust; I will not be afraid.
> What can mortal man do to me? (Psalm 56:3–4).

Biblical illustrations

Am I the only one who feels embarrassed when I read the account of the mother of James and John (Matthew 20:20–22)? Mrs. Zebedee went to Jesus to ask a favor on behalf of her two adult sons. She asked Christ to let her two sons sit on the thrones next to the Son of God.

I cringe every time I hear this doting, interfering mother trying to gain favors for her sons. Jesus simply told her she didn't know what she was asking. He then turned to the brothers and discussed the seriousness of following Him.

Doesn't the thought of this hurt your toes? How many times have we been tempted to pull some strings, wield a little influence and push our children through the right doors? That's because we are attached to parenting and don't know how to step back.

A better illustration is found in the story of Elisha. He had been chosen to minister after Elijah was finished. When the prophet threw his coat over the young man's shoulders, Elisha made one request. He wanted to go and say farewell to his parents.

"Elisha then left his oxen and ran after Elijah. 'Let me kiss my father and mother good-by,' he said, 'and then I will come with you.'

" 'Go back,' Elijah replied. 'What have I done to you?' " (1 Kings 19:20).

It is one thing to hold on to our grown children in fear and anxiety. The opposite is to set them free to fly under the careful eye of the God we serve and worship.

Are we to be left alone?

One of the main fears found among children is separation. They want to know if Mom and Dad are going to return. They also want to know what will happen to them if their parents die or are divorced. Called separation anxiety, it bothers most children to some extent.

Adults suffer from the same fear. Understandably, we don't like to see the people we are fond of move away from us. That makes us feel insecure and uneasy. We want our family members close enough to grab hold of when we need them, like security blankets.

The parents who feel this the most are traditional mothers. They stayed home, raised children, cooked, and attended PTA meetings. Now they are in their fifties and their structure has moved away. What are they to do now? Are they to sit home alone and wait for their adult children to call?

At the same time Mom starts to see Dad's health slide. His knees pop, his back aches, he is taking two or three medications. More and more of the names on their phone list end with M.D.

She notices more entertainers and politicians dying in their fifties and she has to wonder how long before she might be living alone. Separation anxiety begins to fog up the windows of her life.

If this traditional mother doesn't soon discover new meaning in her life, she may find herself fighting loneliness on several fronts. Eventually she may be lonely on all sides.

Each parent has watched loneliness eat away at the elderly, and the prospect is frightening. They know that both traditional and modern parents can be victims of isolation and emptiness.

Paul Welter says in his book about meaning, "Meaninglessness, however, takes the center stage in grief if the loss represents the control value in life."[1] If child-rearing has been our main activity, our main hope and our major addiction, their departure has to give us a deep feeling of loss. That loss will result in the pain of loneliness if we don't make other arrangements.

Quick and easy fixes

Many of us middle-aged parents refuse to see separation as a dilemma. We think life will continue as

---

1. Paul Welter, *Counseling and the Search for Meaning*, 88.

smooth as a marble; the kids will move out and that will be that. We see it as natural and everybody does it.

This denies the facts. The physical loss of our children will take some serious adjustments. If those changes don't take place gradually, they will have to take place abruptly after the fact. Abrupt changes are awkward and often misunderstood. Those adjustments can and frequently do cause trouble in the family.

Once we accept the fact that family change is coming like a train, we have to make the adjustments. Those alterations may be very difficult and should be started early.

Should the parent look for a spiritual ministry, get a part-time job, do charity work, travel, get a boat, adopt a refugee family, begin an exercise regime, teach a class at the mission, become a good neighbor to the elderly, fall in love all over again or what? We must find some of the meaning which we formally vested in our children. It takes time and effort to find our new niche, and some parental veterans don't want to exert the energy. They want to find an easy fix. Thirty years of watching soap operas and football games is not a good solution.

It's interesting to watch the people in our small town make the adjustment. They join clubs, find friends to take to coffee, go on trips, find jobs, redo their houses, learn German, go on mission projects. Others grouse a lot, complain about uncaring children, get divorced, become bitter, and basically disintegrate.

Many of us find these the happiest, most contented years of our lives. But this comes about through dedicated work. Others experience misery and disillusionment. Most of us have a choice.

Why Do I Feel Like Nobody When I'm Not Parenting?

It's something like retiring from the Navy at age forty-two. If you aren't going to sail on destroyers and aircraft carriers anymore, what are you going to do for the next thirty years? Retired sailors can't sit around and feel like nobody the rest of their lives. They can't say, "If I'm not a sailor anymore, I might as well give up."

Some parents do that. Some wives who couldn't have children or couldn't have any more children quit living. We have all seen them. They felt defeated, useless, and had little motivation to go on. Some women believed they were put on earth to reproduce and when that was no longer a possibility, they lost all sense of purpose.

Here is the problem: if the purpose of life is to multiply, then most of us have now run out of purpose halfway through the race. Then we get nervous because we don't know how to deal with the rest of the course.

Our major defining point

The people in our town still do it. They define us by our children. "Oh, you're June's mom," or "You must be Jim's dad."

Many of them still call us either Mary or Jim or June instead of our real names because they know we are Colemans. They saw our children in sports, plays, music, academics, choir, or at work, and that's the way they identify us. We have lives of our own but many do not see us that way. To them we will always be so and so's mother or father.

That's all right. It's a privilege to be their parents. The problem arises when we also see ourselves mainly as parents. If we do, we could feel like nothing when we aren't parenting.

And if not parenting means I am nobody, I must hang on to parenting as long as I possibly can. But I cannot allow myself to become nothing. That kind of thinking creates havoc for millions of "empty nesters." The logic falls apart and leaves us to create problems simply because we have incorrectly emphasized parenting.

How would someone describe you?

If I had never met you and asked a friend of yours to describe you, what would he say? I might say, "I need to go and talk to this person; what can you tell me about him before I go?" How would your friend respond?

Certainly he would say you are a wonderful person. But would he add: "She is a good gardener."

"He is a great golfer."

"She is a terrific parent."

"He is a hard worker."

Or would your friend say several things about you. For instance, "She has a part-time job; she loves her family; she teaches a class on Tuesdays; she loves to play tennis; she sings in the choir; she likes people."

Would he reply, "She is a wonderful parent," and that would end the description? If that's likely, there is reason to be concerned.

My office desk has six legs; it could lose a leg and still manage to stand. But if a desk has just one large pedestal in the middle, it is totally dependent on that pedestal. Should it be removed, the desk can no longer function like a desk.

Children do not make us people. Children are not our full reason for living. Children are not our total purpose. If all of our children move to India, we would not cease to be complete, vital people. We remain an essential member of the family of God no matter what role we now play in our children's lives.

The first twenty-five or thirty years of our lives may have been heavily defined by our parenting responsibilities. How would you like the next thirty years to be defined?

It's not too late

Today's newspaper tells the story of two women who began graduate school at Harvard. One is twenty-six years old. The other is fifty-four. It turns out they have known each other for over a quarter century. The two are mother and daughter, and they are both reaching out to fulfill their dreams.

First of all, none of us should be defined by what we do. We are real people no matter what our activities. People confined to wheelchairs in nursing homes are one-hundred-percent human beings. Our value will not change because our activities change.

Second, where do you want to go from here? The opportunities are almost limitless. Hobbies, school, careers, promotions, and adventures are everywhere.

Look at some great examples:

- Ronald Reagan became president in his late sixties.
- Moses started agitating Pharaoh when he was eighty.
- Winston Churchill became Prime Minister when he was sixty-six.
- Grandma Moses, the elderly painter, lived to be one hundred.
- Dave Thomas, the founder of Wendy's restaurants, graduated from high school at age sixty.
- My friend Shirley published her first book after her last child left home.

Our neglected gifts

When we were younger, there was a great emphasis on discovering our talents, gifts, and abilities. Most of us were looking for lifelong career decisions or we were trying to figure out where we fit in the local church. There seems to be less discussion of gifts and talents among the forty-five to sixty-year-old group. In one church I attended this age group moved up to the "graveyard" Sunday school class where they waited for Social Security to kick in.

Take a fresh look at 1 Corinthians 12. Ask God to go through the passage with you and highlight certain verses that might apply to your mature years. What spiritual gifts could you use to strengthen and minister to other Christians?

As you read, keep these guidelines in mind.

1. *All of us are necessary and important to other believers.*

That's part of who we are. We aren't former parents or ex-parents; rather we are always vital parts in the body of Christ. Some churches have developed programs to train fifty- and sixty-year-olds. We are ready to move up to the next stage of our lives and we have plenty of gifts that other Christians need.

A United States senator has announced that he will leave the Senate and fulfill a longstanding commitment to his church.

"The body is a unit, though it is made up of many parts; and though all its parts are many, they form one body" (1 Corinthians 12:12).

2. *Open our hearts to the possibilities.*

The Christian community needs a wide variety of gifts and helps to keep in healthy condition. The Scriptures mention a few gifts with an almost endless array of possibilities.

Read verses 8–10 and 27–30 of 1 Corinthians 12. Does God want to use your gift of faith or knowledge or healing or teaching or administration to benefit others?

Match a need you see with an ability or interest you believe God has given you and go to work. The person who teaches Bible or English to a small group of prison inmates may be doing exactly that.

Be willing to exercise your new gifts. When you were twenty-two and starting your family, you probably knew little about children. Now that they are grown you might want to discuss child-rearing at the local family shelter. Your spiritual gifts may have grown as a result of considerable experience at work and at home.

3. *Give the greatest gift.*

Fortunately not every gift is dependent on manual dexterity or a master's degree. Many children as well as adults need to see the gift of love demonstrated by a mature Christian. We can all use that exalted gift.

"But eagerly desire the greater gifts. And now I will show you the most excellent way. If I speak in the tongues of men and of angels, but have not love, I am only a resounding gong or a clanging cymbal" (1 Corinthians 12:31–13:1).

Former President and Mrs. Carter are great examples. They have not only raised their children, but they have also completed their careers. It would be easy to spend their time writing books, accepting honors, fishing, and doting on their families.

Instead, they have reached out to use their considerable gifts. As Christians they attend peace conferences, monitor democratic elections, build houses, and participate in numerous other causes. They are deeply involved in church and denominational efforts, living out their Christian commitment in new and adventurous ways.

Our identity gap widens

Even if we want to lose ourselves in our children's identity, it becomes more and more difficult. There is a great gap between parent and grown child. Our children's attitudes, values, and lifestyles are far different from our own.

All of us have separated from our own parents. Fifty years ago we came from smaller communities; change was slower; morals were closer; there was less mobility, even fewer ideas. It was far more likely that we would grow up to share our parents' outlook.

Today our children's attitudes toward government, marriage, child-rearing, finances, housework, careers, and education are far different from our feelings at their age. They even feel at ease about switching churches and denominations (and presently 24 percent of those in our children's generation have made such a change).

In days gone by the son often worked the same farm or at the same factory or foundry as his father. A daughter would do almost exactly what her mother and grandmother had done. There was predictability and stability. Acorns didn't take root very far from the tree.

Now, father is an insurance agent and his son plays drums in a Christian rock band. Mother works part-time at Wal-Mart and her daughter is a dentist in Fresno. Their other daughter volunteers at an ecology group stuffing envelopes to help save the ozone.

It's tough to lose ourselves in our children's dreams if they are skydiving in Colorado or marching to save the whales. That's simply not us.

Let's do it our way. Let's become ourselves. Let's find where and how God wants to use us. None of us has to be lost in our children.

Don't Fight the Facts

Have you seen the ads on television about the new skin cream? The one that promises to remove wrinkles and make you look fifteen years younger. There should be a law! Finally, we accept the fact that middle-age has arrived, and along comes this product. It tells us to fight the feeling and pretend we are thirty-five again.

Buy it if you want to, but I'm glad to be my age. I don't want to dye my hair, tuck anything, cover my liver spots, and buy a motorcycle. I worked hard to get here and I'm going to enjoy it.

There's no more pressure to look like a movie star, compete with the twenty-five-year-olds or wear a waistline four sizes too small. I want to be me. That's all I ever really wanted to be and it's time to make my dreams come true.

In order to be ourselves, we have to move on and let go. If pressed, most of us would say we aren't interested in parenting forever. We want to graduate to the next plateau. But despite our best intentions, we remain closet parents while we insist that we aren't.

A mother in Arizona was visiting her two daughters. The girls shared an apartment while one was finishing college and the other had taken a job.

Their mother would never dream of telling them what to do. She was done with trying to run their lives. While she might be generous with praise, she was a million miles away from any form of criticism.

But the girls noticed their mother had a peculiar habit. As she sat on the couch and visited, she would automatically reach into her purse and draw out her handkerchief. Without changing the subject or skipping a beat, Mother would dust off the neglected coffee table.

The girls watched in horror as their mother silently cleaned house for two daughters in their mid-twenties.

This was clearly something their mother didn't intend to do. She certainly never would have dusted the coffee table in a friend's house. But Mother knew the girls needed this. Torn between her respect for these young adults and their obvious need for help, Mother reverted to her nurturing instincts and practically brought both of her daughters to tears.

It isn't enough for us to chant:

"I don't try to control my grown children."

"I don't try to control my grown children."

"I don't try to control my grown children."

If in fact we do try to control our grown children, that's a sign that we have learned what to say but we are denying the facts.

She kept trying

I saw a movie recently in which the mother of a grown daughter is obviously unhappy with the way her offspring has turned out. Unable or unwilling to bite her tongue, Mother continuously tries to prod, change, control, and manipulate the daughter who is in her late thirties.

The daughter is a divorced mother, clearly overweight, insecure, and at war with her family. At a social occasion the aging mother removes a cookie from her daughter's hand and says, "Let's allow the thin people to eat those."

That kind of rude, blatant rejection naturally sent the daughter on another eating binge.

Whatever mistakes the mother had made in the past, the daughter seems determined to repeat them. Her unwillingness to step aside and stop parenting continues to erode and destroy any hope that the two might have a meaningful relationship.

Turtle necks

Nature tells us that even turtles know when to stick their necks out and when to pull them back inside the shell for safety. Imagine that a turtle becomes disoriented and starts sticking its neck out at the wrong times. Sooner or later the timid tortoise is going to get into a terrible mess simply because it is flunking neck-sticking.

Many of us were good at getting involved when our children were young. We practiced the art of plunging our necks into places where it definitely belonged, especially in those shaky teen years. Now the true test is whether we have enough sense to withdraw our necks at the right times.

All of us have good advice to give and we wish our children were smart enough to listen to us. We have tons of experience and wisdom coming out of our ears. The tricky part is to know how to keep it to ourselves.

It's like President Truman said on the subject of giving advice to children. He said the best way to give advice to children is to find out what they want to do and advise them to do it.

How much to intercede

Your twenty-eight-year-old daughter calls to say that she has car trouble. She has taken the vehicle to a nearby garage. The mechanic told her he could do it, and the price could range from $200 to $300.

Why is she calling her parents? She wants her parents to call the garage and make sure the price stays close to $200. In the parents' eagerness to help, they do exactly what they did when the child was twelve. They intercede.

The temptation is too great. How could a parent resist doing a good deed for his child?

Years ago I was putting a business deal together when I received a phone call. The voice on the other end was a well-meaning mother I had met somewhere along the way. Her grown, college-graduate son was interested in becoming part of this venture. She wanted to make sure I knew about his excellent qualifications.

My natural thought was, "Why doesn't the son call? Is he paralyzed with fear? Is he afraid he will mispronounce my name? Does he drool over the phone? Why did Mom call?"

In her willingness to help she seems to be preventing him from growing up. If he cannot assert himself at his age, when will he be able to speak up for himself?

Your heart goes out to the mother who loves her son so much; but look at the damage she does. Good intentions and noble goals are not enough. Doting parents can make a mess of a situation even when their intent is the highest ideal.

A little introspection helps

The Bible encourages us to take a stern look at who we are and what we are doing. The unexamined life is barely worth living. It is too easy to deceive ourselves and hurt others because we refuse to face up to what we are doing.

On the one hand we insist that we let them lead their own lives. On the other hand we stir the pot and create havoc.

Let's ask ourselves a few questions and check them out with the Scriptures.

1. *Are we interfering in our adult child's life and can't admit it?*

"The wisdom of the prudent is to give thought to their ways, but the folly of fools is deception" (Proverbs 14:8).

What does this passage mean? Smart people are willing to check out their behavior and give it an honest look. Maybe our words say one thing while our conduct speaks an entirely different language.

The question is, are we still parenting our children and feeding our attachment? Don't simply slough off that challenge without looking closely at the way we act toward them.

The author of Proverbs says: The most foolish thing any fool can do is to live in deception. That's what denial is. Denial says we have a problem with it but we won't admit that, not even to ourselves.

Self-deception prevents the Holy Spirit from working with us and it stops us from working with our own problems.

2. *Can we gain self-control?*

When our children were little we needed to exercise considerable control over them. We wiped noses, told them when to go to the bathroom, made them eat green things, and insisted that they sit still.

We may have felt unsuccessful in controlling our children, but did we ever try! Control is always an issue in families. Hopefully we released control bit by bit until they were ready to leave home.

Now it is time to draw back and concentrate on self-control. Grown children must control themselves, and their parents have to take their hands off.

Fortunately, self-control is a major product derived from the fruit of the Spirit.

"But the fruit of the Spirit is love, joy, peace, patience, kindness, goodness, faithfulness, gentleness and self-control" (Galatians 5:22–23).

Most of us feel out of control sometimes. Either we can't tame our minds or our bodies or our behavior. The Scripture promises that God's Spirit can help us gain self-control as we surrender to that Spirit.

The parent who says, "I can't help it, but I keep interfering in my children's lives" might be correct. He needs the Holy Spirit to help him pull back inside his boundaries.

3. *The difference between busy and busybody.*

A mother said, "It seems like I have more to do than ever. Those married kids of mine need so much help. I am over at their place half the time."

Who could fault a good woman like that? She sacrifices greatly to make life easier for her poor, struggling married children.

The woman certainly is busy enough, but maybe she fails to see the difference between busy and busybody. Paul explains a clear distinction in his second letter to the Thessalonians. "We hear that some among you are idle. They are not busy; they are busybodies" (3:11).

Some grown children need the help of parents. Who can fault us if we help paint a little here or fix a water pump there? That sounds loving and civil.

The problem arises when we become intrusive, overbearing, controlling, or take up all their time. We can either be busy helping with genuine needs or we can be busybodies and stick our noses into their every move.

"A finger in every pie" refers to a busy person. When a dozen of those pies belong to our grown children, we may create trouble.

Ask your spouse or friend

Parents who are too involved in their children's lives will have trouble seeing it. That's understandable.

Ask a fish if it's wet. How would it know?

Ask a snail if it's slow. How does it gauge speed?

Ask a bird if it is afraid of heights. It won't know what you're talking about.

Ask a graduate parent if he is too deeply involved in his children's lives and you could either get a blank look or a flat denial. Parents would be wise to take a daring step and ask their spouse or a close friend how they see it.

Be honest! Tell them what you do, when you do it, and how often you do it. Let them respond. They can supply mile-markers to show you where you are. If they suggest you cut back, hold up or ease off, maybe they should be taken seriously.

A good friend might hurt our feelings by telling us to back off from our children, but we can take that from someone we respect.

"Faithful are the wounds of a friend" (Proverbs 27:6).

On a number of occasions I have asked my friends if they thought I had gone too far. When they have said I was going to extremes, I took it very seriously and toned down my involvement.

The verbal check

One way to gauge if we are still trying to control is to take the word test. Are we still saying the same things to our twenty-four-year-old that we said when he was sixteen? If we are, we may be stuck in suspended parenthood.

When was the last time you said:

"Be careful driving home now."

"Are you eating right?"

"Are you taking anything for that cold?"

"Don't let them push you around."

"You had better leave those desserts alone."

"You want me to call them for you?"

"How are your grades coming?"

"You don't even wear a scarf."

"Here, eat some more."

"Go, demand your money back."

"Here, comb your hair."

If our sayings for fourteen-year-olds and twenty-four-year-olds are interchangeable, this might be a clue. Maybe we refuse to recover from parenting and we don't want to admit it.

It's your life

Don't you wish you had five dollars for every time you said, "It's your life"? We have always wanted to turn our children's lives over to them. But despite our best intentions, we have never been able to cast them from the shore.

We have the right words. We pass the vocabulary test. Unfortunately we may still be failing the reality test. That's easy to do. A typical conversation will go like this:

"She has a job now," says Father. "I think it's time we put the car in her name."

"I know," Mother speaks. "She needs to stand on her own two feet."

"Why don't we just pay the insurance for a while till she gets settled?" Father says.

"That's a good idea," Mother agrees, "and I'll pay for her tags out of the groceries."

"Let's not get carried away," warns Father. "But I can see my way to pay half of the car payment, but not for long."

"I feel good about what we're doing. I mean about making her more independent," Mother says.

"You bet," Father says. "And we need to tell her what we've decided. I'll tell her right after the first of the year."

The withdrawal symptoms are hard on parents. We shake and worry over how to let go.

The Battle Against Gravity

Did middle age creep up on us? We didn't notice our eyes slowly developing bags, or see those wrinkles inching across our foreheads. We grew old a day at a time. I think it was Thursday. Our family was eating supper that evening when I decided to make clever conversation.

"June and I cleaned out the car this afternoon," I announced with considerable self-satisfaction. With the smile still fresh on my face, Pat, my wife, replied, "It doesn't matter; I think the piano should stay where it is."

Without any further explanation she went back to eating her peas and breaded squash.

While we each looked puzzlingly at one another, I began to ask myself what had just happened. None of the options seemed pretty.

Perhaps Pat had totally lost her hearing, which meant we were doomed to spend the rest of our lives in an over-heated living room shouting at each other. I conjured up visions of her sitting with a ram's horn stuck in her ear leaning into conversations trying to pick up every second word.

Another possibility was that her arteries were as stiff as licorice sticks, which meant that I would have to hold her hand periodically and ask if she recognized me. Apparently neither was completely the case, and Pat goes on with a fairly normal life.

I don't mention this to evoke sympathy but only to give you some bearing as to what is happening at our age. We aren't facing old age. If we carried canes, people would rush to our sides and help us up the stairs. Friends would serve us soft foods when we visit. Our problem is middle age, and few people seem to understand anything about the creeping sagging bodies we harbor.

It would be easy to blame our troubles on our imaginations. Something psychosomatic. But it has to be age. We can see it clearly in our friends. They are starting to go to the hospital for hernias and hemorrhoids. These are not the ailments of youth. Young people break legs playing football. My friends attract sitting illnesses. It hurts them to cough.

We pass our evenings in hospitals watching friends adjust slowly on chair cushions. Young people are playing softball and throwing frisbees. We are reading get well cards and trying to say something good about having stitches on our private parts. Life has lost its zip.

God created backyards for people with weak arches and stretch slacks. Reputable taxpayers sit in the backyard, drink tea, and fantasize about interest rates. Mountains and streams were made for young people in sweatbands and shorts.

These are a few of life's pleasures that are lost on youth. It will take them thirty years to understand some of God's greatest gifts, like

> soft music
> films of World War II
> Scrabble by the fireplace
> Bob Hope
> slides
> George Beverly Shea
> Wild Kingdom
> golf

And it's a waste of time to try to explain. Any generation that enjoys mountain biking and skiing is too far gone even to appreciate Dragnet reruns. That's just the way it is, ma'am.

It isn't that we are ready for a visiting nurse or extra strength prune juice. There are plenty of miles left in these rounding shoulders and popping knees. Hopefully decades. But we do notice that the insurance programs advertised on television now target our age group. "Sixty days in the hospital could cost you thousands of dollars in uncovered bills—bills you must pay for" has my name written all over it.

We are pictured in the Scriptures

Now that the children are gone, Ecclesiastes 12 starts to take on personal meaning for us. When we look in the mirror we can see each verse come to life before our eyes.

1. Verse 3 speaks of "strong men [who] stoop." I'm actually getting shorter. My stepson rubs my head for good luck.

2. Verse 3 says "[my] grinders cease because they are few." Those are my discolored, plastic-studded teeth he is talking about. I'm popping denture tablets into a plastic cup every night.

3. Verse 3 tells me the "windows grow dim." Bifocals tilt my head up and down like a toy waterbird when I read labels on the store shelves.

4. In verse 5 I am becoming the grasshopper who "drags himself along." Our last trip to the Colorado mountains showed me what a poky grasshopper I have become. During the first three days walking the trails, half of my time was spent leaning against a rock, breathing like a runaway locomotive.

It's not as though we are fulfilling prophecy, but it is obvious that we are walking into our destiny. The old body will slow down, cough, wheeze, and eventually give up. It's good to know that we enter the last third of our lives (the Lord willing) as part of the family of God, secure in the person of his Son, Jesus Christ.

How dare I make fun of us aging, white-haired elders? The author of Ecclesiastes thought of it first. If he can poke fun at my disappearing teeth, I guess I should, too.

You try to ignore Wrinkleville and it's tough. We are getting compliments usually reserved for nursing-home residents. I spoke at a conference recently and afterwards a man with gray sideburns told me, "That was a terrific message. It's so encouraging to know that you older guys stay so current."

There must be some truth to it. Not long ago people said I looked like Teddy Roosevelt. Today they compare me to Wilford Brimley. I'm as surprised as anyone that my mustache has turned blond. It really is blond.

Let us go gently into the late afternoon of life and enjoy the sunset. We don't want to compete with hang gliders and jiggling joggers. Not that we aren't vigorous and healthy. It's just that we don't want to compete forever. Middle age may be the first time we have been comfortable with ourselves. Now some healthnik wants us to wear eyebrow cream.

Not that we have folded up and died. In fact, Pat and I decided to take a marathon walk one summer. We weren't in a fit of competition, mind you; it was simply something the two of us wanted to try. Early one morning we took off walking to York, Nebraska, twenty-three miles away.

What a great idea. We would walk over on the paved road, spend the night in a motel and walk back the next day. The motel, rather than a tent, was our salute to graying temples. We had earned the right to a flat bed.

The first twenty miles were almost a pleasure. We stopped at two gas stations to gulp cold drinks, sandwiches, and candy bars. The life of the modern adventurer was exactly our speed. But what we hadn't counted on were the last three miles. Our thighs began to swell up like bags of golf balls in wet leather. We wanted to sit down and rest but we weren't sure our legs would bend. If we did manage to get down, there was no promise we could ever rise again.

In a desperate effort to gain strength, I took out a bag of M&M's as I staggered onward. Though they tasted terrific, they refused to slide down my parched throat.

There I stood on Highway 34 spitting out the candy I was counting on to save my life. Granted it wasn't exactly the Jenkin's Walk Across America, but it was a start. (I couldn't write a book about our experience, but maybe a snappy pamphlet would do.)

The next day we trekked home like zombies in a B movie. The bottoms of our feet hurt so badly we hated to get off the pavement when cars came. My legs screamed each time I asked them to move sideways toward the shoulder of the road. I turned to Pat and cheerfully asked what her biggest surprise was about the trip. Dourly she answered, "The pain."

The last six miles of the walk were the hardest of the forty-six. Only mindless drudgery kept us going. Near home people who knew us drove by and then came back, not unlike vultures. A nurse we knew stopped and said, "Bill, you don't look well."

By some peculiar gift from God we made it home that night and sat like mannequins on the couch. The only way to get off the couch was to slide onto the floor and then climb up the arms of the furniture. But why do that? There was no place we had the energy to go.

Don't call us back to youthful conformity. Middle-agers have the right to live in their own world. Let us go nuts at our own speed.

If we had allowed youth-types to talk us out of the trip, we would have missed some of the wonders of nature: the smell of gas fumes, empty beer cans, dead ermine, loose pages from an old "Playboy," an angry dog climbing a fence, overcast skies that threatened to pour on us.

We communed with God and breathed carbon monoxide on the oil-soaked highways. And God scratched His head and worried about us.

But I figure this was the way Moses got his big break. He spent forty years in Egypt and the next forty living in the desert. (There weren't many highways available.) Then at middle age—eighty for him—God decided to use the graying shepherd. Not a bad deal. The first two-thirds of my life are spent—maybe more. But with my experience there might be some great openings available. We aren't interested in acting like teenagers. But if God gives us twenty-five more years, we might as well get in gear and use them to serve him—crow's-feet and all.

Jacob and the
Coat of Many Colors

Remember when our children used to ask, "Who do you like best, me or Jody?" or "Owen is your favorite child, isn't he?" We would emphatically deny that we had a favorite and insist that we loved each one equally.

A child would like to know that he is loved most. He wants to be someone special, just a notch above the rest.

Many of us as parents hemmed and hawed around trying to come up with a good answer. For one thing we didn't know how to reply. For another, sometimes we wondered if maybe we did have a favorite child but we didn't dare admit it.

None of us can afford the luxury of having a favorite child. Instinctively we know that. But sometimes we were drawn to the child that was most like us. Other times we especially appreciated the child who was the most compliant and was quick to do what she was told.

Smart parents refuse to have a favorite. Though naturally drawn to one child, they fight the temptation. No matter what the child's behavior or disposition, wise parents work hard at accepting each child evenly. It is hard but it is necessary.

Use what we learned

Most of us learned lessons about favoritism the hard way. But we did learn. If we had it to do over again, we would be smarter.

Now that our children have grown we have the opportunity to benefit from our experience. The situation is very similar.

We cannot afford the luxury of having a favorite adult child.

Our potential to do great damage is still there if we sway or swing toward one person and "crown" him as a special child. It doesn't work any better when the children are in their forties than it did when they were in grade school.

Not treated the same

Some parents are so afraid of treating one adult child better than the other that they ignore all of them. That's not the solution. We can go camping in Idaho with one child and not go with all four children. It would be foolish to avoid activities unless all eight adults, eight grandchildren, two cats, and the goldfish can go along.

Don't keep a calendar or a stopwatch and add up how much time you spend with each. The key is thoughtfulness. Keep each adult child on your mind. Look for ways to interact. Find situations to share. Be caring without being intrusive. If you sense that your attention has shifted too far away from someone, correct it by moving toward him.

The important question is:

"Am I making good contact with this adult child?"

The question is *not*:

"Am I making too much good contact with the other adult children?"

Make constructive contact with each adult child. Don't decide to cut off Child B because you don't see Child C enough.

Time and distance

These are big factors in determining how we interact with an adult child. We might attend a baseball game with a family that lives in the same city as we do. But the ball game 1,200 miles away will have to go on without us. The question isn't, how do we make that up to the family far away? The goal is to ask how we can interact in that family or individual's own peculiar circumstances.

That frees us up to treat everyone as a special person.

The family far away may need phone calls, videos, tapes, letters, and packages. These might not be appropriate responses to the family living in town.

Where Jacob failed

One of the most interesting family stories in the Bible concerns Jacob, the patriarch, and his grown children.

By the time Joseph was seventeen years old, father Jacob had declared him as his favorite child and had begun to dote on him excessively.

Genesis 37:3 tells us, "Now Israel loved Joseph more than any of his other sons, because he had been born to him in his old age."

We have all seen it happen. Joseph was a tag-a-long kid. His parents were aging and probably lacked the energy to set limits, discipline, and follow through with little Joseph. They treated him more like a grandchild than a child. Grandparents are supposed to spoil their grandchildren, but parents shouldn't.

Not only was Joseph his father's favorite, but Jacob made no attempt to disguise it. His friends, his neighbors, and his children knew which child he liked the best.

Jacob even gave Joseph a coat that made him stand out above the others. The colors may have been prominent or the sleeves may have been extra large or the material may have been especially fine. Perhaps all three were true (Genesis 37:3).

It was as if Jacob had bought Joseph a huge, new motorcycle while the rest of the sons tooled around on mopeds. The gift was extra special, and everyone knew it.

The fact that Jacob picked out a favorite and made that obvious caused tremendous pain to his family. The sons tried to kill Joseph and eventually sold him into slavery. By the grace of God the situation was turned into good, but everyone went through enormous agony over the problem.

As a father Jacob was tempted to focus on one child; we all understand that. But he was obligated to hold his favoritism in check. Jacob owed it to everyone involved to get a hold on his feelings and put his priorities in order.

Our focus changes

Don't be surprised if you have a favorite child during the grade school years, a different favorite during junior high or senior high, and another favorite after they all leave home. Favoritism is a tricky business. Compliance, obedience, and living up to expectations have a way of changing like the wind.

The person who "catches our eye" when he is seven may bring us some serious migraines when he reaches seventeen, twenty-seven, or thirty-seven. Others remain "pets" throughout their lifetimes.

Favoritism is too often based on performance. And performance is usually fickle and unpredictable.

How do we resist favoritism?

There are a number of Christian values which could help us stay away from the favoritism trap. They are extremely important and well worth the effort to put them into operation.

First, recognize that every child is a gift from God.

The child who graduates from Harvard is no more a gift from God than the daughter who works at the Quik Shop. The child who attends church is not more special than the one who never does. That isn't the way we naturally feel, but in God's economy every child is special. That includes the two-year-old and the forty-two-year old.

> Sons are a heritage from the LORD,
> children a reward from him (Psalm 127:3).

Our child with the alcohol problem. Our child who is divorced. Our child who is unreliable. Each is still a child, a gift from God.

The unplanned child, the handicapped child, the unemployed child. Each one and every one is special.

Second, impartiality is basic.

None of us is permitted to favor the athlete, the cheerleader, or the valedictorian. All are of equal value by biblical standards. Nor can we show partiality to the slow learner, the sick, or the poor. They are not better than anyone else either.

All of us are of equal value. If we favor the pretty child or dote over the heavy child, in both cases we fail the Bible's concept of value. We are important because God created us in His image and Jesus Christ died for us.

"Do not pervert justice; do not show partiality to the poor or favoritism to the great, but judge your neighbor fairly" (Leviticus 19:15).

Impartiality is fundamental to a healthy love for people.

Third, God does not show favoritism.

Often Christians must think exactly opposite of the world around them. Whether or not others show partiality to certain children, that option still does not belong to us.

There is a godly wisdom that takes the Christian to higher and better standards. That wisdom helps us handle all of our children as equals.

"But the wisdom that comes from heaven is first of all pure; then peace loving, considerate, submissive, full of mercy and good fruit, impartial and sincere" (James 3:17).

Impartiality is an integral part of God's wisdom.

We need all of the encouragement we can get to deal with our grown children evenly. It would be easy to follow our natural instincts. This is one area where God can change the way we think.

Watch their eyes

Make a mental note the next time you ask a parent how his children are doing. When he mentions Cassie, do his eyes light up and his voice rise? When he tells you about Andy, the other child, do his eyes half close as he looks at the ground?

I've noticed that with parents I have talked to. And if I see the different reactions, we can be certain that Cassie and Andy see it, too.

The answer

What do we do if we know we have a favorite adult child? What if we have an order: We like this one best, that one next and the other one third?

We need to ask God to help us have the same attitude as God. He needs to make us aware of our imbalance and help level us off. We have to consciously, deliberately increase our appreciation for the child we may not always care for.

As adults we have the ability to adjust our feelings. If a child doesn't like to shop the way we do, we don't shy away from him; we look for something he does like to do. When one child is rude, we try to work with his rudeness; we don't avoid him because he is rude. If we sense a growing distance between ourselves and one of the children, we make the move toward him. These are signs of maturity. Parents are responsible to make the adjustments.

We don't like everything our children do. But none of us can allow their behavior to drive us away.

Parents should be able to say that they love each of their children. They should be able to point out qualities in each adult child that they find attractive and pleasing. Smart parents concentrate on those things.

Even when our adult children have severe behavior problems, we can still find some aspect to praise. Their good qualities may not offset their bad ones, but we need to acknowledge their assets nevertheless.

Some parents may need to discuss this with the Lord. Tell God that you have trouble seeing the good in one particular adult child (even though others see good in him or her). Ask God to help you highlight that child's good features. Not that we close our eyes to his faults, but that we also accept his strengths. We may need to call for extra spiritual power to accept each adult child.

Tempted to Interfere

Check those that apply:

❏ Have you ever called your twenty-eight-year-old son and reminded him to file his income tax form?
❏ Did you call your married daughter and ask about her finances?
❏ When your son said he didn't want a wooden gate for the top of the stairs, did you order one and have it mailed to his house to protect your grandchild?
❏ When your daughter planned a skiing trip over the Christmas holidays, did you throw a fit?
❏ When you learned that your two-year-old grandson was not enrolled in Sunday school, did you chew out both mother and father?

How do parents know when they are helping and when they are intruding? Most parents mean well. They want to help the people they love. But sometimes in our sincerity we step over the line and become pushy. Love that tries to manipulate, love that tries to control, love that insists on its own way is in danger of going too far. Real love recognizes boundaries and works hard to honor them.

But how do we know when we are helping our adult children and when we are interfering? Let's begin with a few clues.

We know we are helping when . . .

1. *They ask us to lend a hand.*

When they call and invite us over to help paint their dining room, we know we are wanted. That's a fairly good sign that they would like us around. The same is true if they tell us what day they are moving and exactly what time.

2. *They say they miss us.*

A strong clue that we have stayed away too long. It's easy to believe it if they say it. If they are continuously encouraging us to come over for dinner or a birthday party or a housewarming, those invitations are easy to interpret.

3. *They ask for a loan.*

Always risky business, but it is frequently done well. They need a specific amount of money for a specified time. It's best if the details are in writing so everyone is less likely to say later, "But I thought you meant . . . ." Don't push money on them. Keep short accounts and communicate, communicate, communicate.

4. *If they ask advice.*

As nervous parents we wonder when to add our two cents. The safest time is when they ask. Any other time is swollen with danger.

Whether it's child-rearing, sex, finances, vacations, churches or sports, be stingy with advice. Young couples tell us to wait until we are asked.

5. *They ask us to get involved.*

If they need a place to stay for the summer, let them say so. Don't take the initiative away and begin solving all of their problems. Let them spell out how we can best help. Few things are more painful than to have a parent who is quick to solve the wrong problems with the wrong solutions.

Sometimes parents can offer help, but only very gingerly. Our children may bless us for taking the initiative but it's like sleeping in the china cabinet. You could do a lot of damage any way you roll.

Test the waters carefully. Whose ego are you stepping on? Whose plans are you messing with? Never deprive anyone of the thrill of making the last payment on a refrigerator.

Help is never help if it robs someone of his sense of dignity and worth.

How do you know if you are interfering?

1. *They tell you to butt out.*

That's a sure sign. It's hard to misinterpret. Little sayings like, "Leave us alone," "That's our business," and "Please, Mother, I'd rather do it myself" are forceful clues. Unfortunately too many parents ignore what is said by telling themselves, "Oh, they don't really mean it." That's a bit strong-willed.

Take direct statements seriously. Some parents are told not to come around so often and the parents shrug it off. When we ignore what our children say, we are inviting them to become more powerful in their communication.

2. *If they keep turning you down.*

Ask if you can baby-sit the grandchildren for the weekend. If the answer is no, ask again at another time. But if the reply is continuously "no," take a hint. Don't wait for a millstone to hit you in the head.

Be persistent, but don't nag. There's a fine line. It isn't reasonable to keep begging when there obviously isn't any interest.

3. *If you have no other friends.*

Our adult children cannot be our sole support group. Instead of investing our energies into collecting friends our own age, it is sometimes easier to rely on our children. That's a bad sign! Wholesome, middle-aged adults will branch out, take risks, and mix with people in their own bracket.

There is nothing wrong with making our children our friends. The problems come when they are our only friends or even practically our only friends. Adult children can be a safe place to "hang out" but that very safety can prove injurious to everyone involved.

How often do you get together with other friends? How often do you get together with your children and their families? You be the judge of whether that ratio is out of proportion.

4. *If you are actively raising them.*

Millie was the kind of mother who constantly bombarded her son's house because she wasn't finished raising him. Mother wanted to check up on how his job was coming along, if he was paying his bills on time, and whether or not he was eating right.

We dare not do that to adults, especially adults who have moved out and are living with their own families. The temptation is great for many parents, but it almost always is a flashing sign that we are interfering.

Dependable checkpoints

If you are wondering if you interfere too much, pick up your Bible and go over the verses below. These important points are ageless and practical for today's complicated family.

Keep your opinions to a minimum.

Give your children your opinion about politics, clothing styles, the national debt, and the Detroit Tigers. But when it comes to family matters, couple relationships, and child-rearing, swallow hard and keep it to yourself. When asked, venture an opinion, but even then hold back on the reins a little. Opinions are dangerous when it comes to family situations.

"A fool finds no pleasure in understanding but delights in airing his own opinions" (Proverbs 18:2).

Stay out of their quarrels.

That's tough to do. If we are forty, fifty, sixty years old or more, we think we have gobs of wisdom. And frankly we do. But sometimes it is better to back off and leave them alone even if we are asked to get involved.

Backing off is hard because we hate to see our children grapple with their own problems; but it's important. Most of the time they need to settle their own quarrels.

The Bible gives a graphic description of people who butt into other peoples' arguments.

"Like one who seizes a dog by the ears is a passer-by who meddles in a quarrel not his own" (Proverbs 26:17).

If we stop little children from arguing with each other, we slow down their maturing process. The same is true if we interfere with our married children. They need to quarrel, debate, disagree, negotiate, and compromise on their own.

Thank God for the parent who knows when to disappear. The next time we start to wade into someone else's argument, picture that dog, hanging by the ears, legs flailing in every direction, yelping and howling. That vision should stop most of us.

Don't exhaust your family.

Nearly every day Tony knew that when he arrived home after work there would be a message on his answering machine. His mother wanted him to call. What would it be today, he wondered? Would she need her sink fixed, was her window jammed, was the bulb out in her refrigerator?

Tony was sure he knew what she was doing. Rather than have him fix two or three things while he was there, she would string them out and only ask for one each day. She wanted her son to drop by every day and this was her way of getting him there.

And did he resent it? She was clearly interfering with his life and Tony didn't know how to stop it.

The book of Proverbs tells us not to lean too heavily on our families. If we have needs, we should go to our friends also and let them share some of the load. Get a friend to work on the jammed window. Hire someone to spend the day making repairs around the house.

> Do not forsake your friend and the
> friend of your father,
> and do not go to your brother's house
> when disaster strikes you—
> better a neighbor nearby than a
> brother far away (Proverbs 27:10).

We tend to mess up our family members' lives by intruding and asking for too much. That's good advice for brothers, sisters, children, and parents.

"But," someone protests, "I thought that was what families were for." Sometimes they are. Occasionally they are the perfect people to help. The problem arises when we use each other too often. There are many relatives who dread visiting other relatives because they will be expected to fix, repair, and rearrange the house.

Don't complain about how they do things.

Probably none of us see ourselves as complainers, but the fact is that many of us are. We say things that make our children bristle.

"When are you guys going to finish off the room?"

"Haven't you taken the kids to the doctor yet?"

"It sounds to me like you need to get a better paying job."

"Man, you have the worst luck buying cars."

"You hardly ever bring the children over."

"It would be great if couples could attend a family seminar once a year."

"I don't know why you two don't come over more."

Those quotes are just samples. They are a few of the reasons why married couples get uptight when parents and in-laws come to visit. Some relatives don't consider their trips complete unless they drop three or four "suggestions" like stink bombs.

One of the marks of mature Christians is that they are not complainers; they do not complain as a regular habit.

"Do everything without complaining or arguing" (Philippians 2:14).

The passage goes on to say that uncontentious believers shine like stars in the universe; we really stand out if we aren't big complainers.

When our adult children know we are coming to their house, do they anticipate us as if we are sparkling stars? Or do they think, here comes the big dark cloud again.

Sometimes we cross the line and interfere without knowing it. Unintentionally we march in where angels fear to tread. It pays to think through the situation and be wise enough to back off.

Why Our Children Blame Us

After placing the last log in the fireplace, I struck a match and set the kindling aflame. There was nothing to it. I had started fires many times.

In less than a minute, however, a problem became apparent. Smoke was dancing around inside the fireplace and then escaping into the living room. Growing in volume, large dark clouds engulfed the curtains.

Quickly I grabbed the poker and stuck it into the lever which opened the vent. Instantly the smoke found the chimney and rushed upward.

"Pat, Pat!" I yelled. "Where are you?"

Frantically I opened windows and plugged in a wall fan to chase the gray column outside. Mumbling to myself I wondered, "Who did this? Who forgot to open the vent?"

Incredibly, I could almost hear a voice in the room say, "Bill, no one is in the room except you."

How disappointing. Where was my family when I needed someone to blame? My index finger darted out in search of someone to accuse, but the room was empty. What a dirty trick fate had played on me.

Parent-blaming is common

Adult children are presently in a frenzy to blame parents for every quirk, twitch, and disability in their lives. Recently a psychologist said this will be the blame-your-parents-for-everything decade. Especially if your children are in their early twenties, be prepared for a barrage of charges.

Normally they grow out of parent-blaming when they start their own families, but not necessarily. Many young adults well beyond their adolescent years look for parental scapegoats. And too often they are told that their parents are the problem.

Don't be surprised. Don't feel alone. Don't let it drive you to distraction.

Blame is a conscious, overt attempt to make someone else responsible for what is going on in my life. The reasons why we most frequently blame our family members are:

1. They were part of our formative years.
2. They furnished our genes or fabric.
3. They may be near at hand (convenient).
4. They may have to put up with our charges.
5. Family-bashing is popular and acceptable.
6. Family members do affect our behavior.

The great banquet of life

Jesus told the story of a man who was preparing a tremendous banquet and invited a large number to attend. He sent servants out to tell his guests about the great feast.

Three people turned the invitation down; each gave an excuse. The first person had bought a field and needed to go check it out. The second person had purchased five yoke of oxen and he needed to work them.

My favorite is the third excuse. He simply said he had married a wife and couldn't attend (Luke 14:20).

The third man had a built-in excuse, and it's high on the list of male cop-outs. Among men it is one of the most frequently used scapegoats. But it is also a common theme among women.

"I always wanted to be a sheepherder, but my wife won't go along."

"If I had my way we would climb the Himalayas, but Jeanne could never eat yak butter."

"I'd like to go skiing, but of course my husband would never want to do that."

Many of us stand back from the great banquet of life and blame others when we don't attend. Frequently our lives are boring, dead-end, spiritually hollow, and mundane because we have found it convenient to blame others for our own stagnation.

Years ago I realized that blaming others had become a habit with me. I was using my wife as a defense mechanism to escape situations I wanted to avoid. Someone would ask me to bring my family to a park for the day and I would use my wife as an excuse. In reality I didn't want to go to the crummy park but wasn't brave enough to simply say so and accept responsibility for my own decision. The easiest and most cowardly thing to do was blame it on my wife who would never know how I had used her.

If you do it enough, using family members as excuses will readily roll off your tongue. (I did it again just yesterday.)

We major on our parents

Forty-year-old Nathan never went to college. He had thought of going; his father had said he would help him go; but just before the time came, his father went bankrupt.

Today Nathan has a laborer's job and barely ekes out a living. After you know him for a while he will explain his problem to you. His father failed to send him to college. Consequently, as Nathan sees it, he had to give up on life and is now forced to dwell in poverty.

This middle-aged man has an excuse to essentially bail out of life. Is it possible that he prefers that excuse because it allows him to avoid the experiences which he could enjoy? It's more than possible.

That's the choice most of us make, and we make it repeatedly. Do we want to sap our energy looking for someone to blame and continuously blame him? Or do we want to throw off the chains of excuses and dive into reality?

Not many of us are 100 percent excuses or 100 percent experiences. On any given day we might be 80/20 either way. But certainly we should be concerned with our pattern. Do we tend to be excuse people or experience people? If we choose to, we can change that ratio.

This choice is close to the heart of racism. The person who blames his or her misfortunes on people of other races uses them as scapegoats. He looks for a reason for not doing better. Unwilling to look inside, that person searches around and finds a target for his or her frustration. When he finds others who agree that race is the problem, he creates the Big Excuse.

Biblically and socially we reach the premise that every person is responsible for his own behavior. There are exceptions to this, but very few. Usually if someone is considered not responsible for his behavior, we try to put him in a controlled environment where others will provide that responsibility.

Except for extreme cases, our parents may be responsible for much of what came into our lives, but we are now responsible for what we do with it.

In his book *Whatever Became of Sin,* Dr. Karl Menninger made a compelling argument for a return to responsibility.[1] The trend still leans heavily toward finding excuses for all of our behavior.

When Bob married into a family, his new in-laws could see immediately that his behavior was destructive. Quick-tempered, insulting, and inconsiderate, Bob acted like a two-year-old in a china cabinet.

Every group has a peacemaker and in this case it was elderly Aunt Louise. Her advice to the rest of the family was to try and allow for Bob's irritable behavior because he came from a family with alcohol problems.

Aunt Louise meant well, but at what point must Bob take control of his own behavior? He doesn't feel the need to have good experiences because he leans on his miserable excuses.

---

1. Karl Menninger, *Whatever Became of Sin,* 46.

The Scripture and accountability

It is tempting to accept blame when our children try to hand it to us. Unfortunately it doesn't help anyone for us to accept blame which is not rightfully ours. If our children rage, it is still foolish for us to carry burdens which are not our own. Put some biblical passages to work in our lives.

1. *Everyone is accountable for his own behavior.*

Parents influence their children, but each of us is ultimately responsible for ourselves. There may be exceptions in cases of extreme abuse but otherwise we are all accountable for our actions. It is unreasonable for a child to say he can't hold a job because of his parents. A woman can't divorce because her father was a drug dealer.

"So then, each of us will give an account of himself to God" (Romans 14:12).

"Nothing in all creation is hidden from God's sight. Everything is uncovered and laid bare before the eyes of him to whom we must give account" (Hebrews 4:13).

Don't accept guilt for something that you did not cause.

2. *Blame-shifting is dishonest.*

When Adam tried to blame Eve for his sin in the garden, he was dishonest with God. He couldn't have open communication with his heavenly Father because he was hiding behind his wife.

If we allow our children to hide behind us, they will be deceiving themselves. When our children say they didn't go to college because of their parents, don't accept the blame. When they say we helped cause their early divorce, don't carry that load. Blame-shifting is dishonest and harmful.

"The man said, 'The woman you put here with me—she gave me some fruit from the tree, and I ate it' " (Genesis 3:12).

3. *Blame-shifting is destructive.*

Grown children cannot deal with their personal problems as long as their parents carry the responsibility. She doesn't have to get a job if she says her parents made her unemployable. He doesn't have to pay his bills if he says his parents made him undependable.

Blame-shifting destroys the ability to function. We do others a terrible injury if we accept blame that is not ours.

Ask Cain and Abel.

Cain shifted the blame to his brother Abel and killed him. Instead of facing up to his own failure before God, Cain acted as if it were Abel's fault. That's destructive behavior.

And after he murdered his brother, Cain didn't want to accept responsibility for anything.

"Then the LORD said to Cain, 'Where is your brother Abel?'

" 'I don't know,' he replied. 'Am I my brother's keeper?' " (Genesis 4:9).

But not everyone does it. Some brave people stand up and say, "I won't live on blame. I will not blame my spouse, my children, my boss, another race, or anyone else. I will break the cycle and take responsibility for my own actions."

A pregnant girl explained to me how her parents had caused this untimely conception. They failed to adequately warn her about sex; they failed to instruct her about contraceptives; they failed to hug her enough; they failed to provide better living conditions.

All of that was probably true. They were imperfect parents who felt embarrassed to discuss this and several other important subjects. Still I was tempted to interrupt and ask the indelicate question, "But you are the one who had sex, aren't you?"

A balanced view of family

Immaturity tends to say that family members are good or bad. In most cases they are actually a bit of both. Unfortunately the habit of blaming is in vogue and holding on tenaciously. When we ask groups of adults to describe their feelings about their parents, their responses are highly negative. Part of the reason may be because one negative feeling or memory seems to drown out ten positive feelings or memories.

A twenty-five-year-old man was in trouble with the law and was pressed to seek a counselor. The counselor met a couple of times with him and then asked the man to contact his parents and bring them.

Eager to cooperate, his parents attended the scheduled session. At that meeting the counselor proceeded to explain that the purchase of a summer cabin twelve years ago was the major cause of the son's problems. Because he was taken from his friends for a month or two each year, he developed a resentment for his parents and thus became maladjusted.

I wasn't in the session and don't know what was said. But when I heard the story, I wondered, "Did anybody mention the benefits of this cabin? The togetherness, the fishing, the memories, the potential friends at the lake? Did anyone discuss the parents' love and industry and ability to provide?"

On the surface it sounds like Dad and Mom gave it a good shot and the son is using the cabin to blame his parents. And the counselor seems quite content to shovel all that guilt in the parents' direction. What needs are best being served here?

None of us is blameless. We must assume that all family members interact with less than perfection. But the lack of perfection is not enough to send our personalities into a permanent quirk.

The Bible tells us parents are the pride of their children (Proverbs 17:6). In a balanced view of the family, we can admit that most parents have been positive contributors to our well-being. Occasionally they are completely injurious to our existence, but not usually. When we can, where we can, we need to acknowledge the good which our parents have supplied.

Accept real guilt. Apologize, ask forgiveness, tell God what you have done. But never accept every wild accusation that your children might toss your way.

We Can't Hide Behind
Our Children

Ted and Linda knew it would happen and they hated to see it come. For twenty-five years they had used their children as shields. Whenever one of them felt a big need to talk about something serious, the other one would pick up a child and hide behind him.

If Ted felt like their love life was the pits, the moment he began to discuss the subject Linda would grab a child. "Oh, Sandy needs a ride to Girl Scouts." She would grab the girl's coat and force her out the back door. "Can't we talk about this later?" Linda smiled as she scurried toward the family car.

There were a lot of important things they never got around to saying because the children were too convenient. They used the children so often that they weren't even aware they were doing it.

"I'd love to rent a cabin this summer," Linda beamed.

"Great idea," Ted agreed, "but this year Kevin has to go to band camp and it costs a bundle. Next summer let's get the cabin for two weeks and make up for it."

But guess what. They didn't go next year either. Sandy needed dental work.

The fact was that Ted and Linda had a great deal of friction between them. Their relationship was restless and rough. There were too many areas they never got around to smoothing out.

Now the prospect loomed large that when their last child moved out they would lose their shields. How were they going to talk, share, and resolve difficulties? They weren't used to that and the prospects made them nervous.

On the other hand we know a couple we'll call Bob and Brenda. They could hardly wait to be left alone. They had places to go and things to do. They had popcorn to make, weekend trips to take, plans to discuss, projects at home, feelings to shore up. They wanted the family room to themselves. They wanted to use their own car for a change.

Bob and Brenda didn't worry about losing their child shield. They weren't hiding behind it anyway.

Most of us are probably a mixture of these two couples. Sometimes we hide from each other and other times we are wide open and receptive. When the last child leaves we need to make as much adjustment as possible to become sharing, supportive, and close.

The big shift

When the final bedroom empties, when the last tuition is paid, when the telephone is no longer tied up, your life will change. Count on it.

You will no longer stay up late waiting for one more teenager to come home.

When your spouse invites you to go out this weekend, you no longer have to decline and say that the kids have a program scheduled.

When she wants a patio on the back of the house, you won't have to say that your daughter needs a dress.

When she suggests you attend a couple's seminar, you won't protest that the youth group needs a chaperon.

When you want to sit together on the couch with the lights down low, you don't have to worry about the kid's barging in.

Neither can you put off going back to school because the children might need you.

The barriers are coming down and the big shifts are on their way. Even widowed or divorced parents can no longer use their children as excuses. Our lives are becoming different and we must decide if it's going to be for better or for worse.

Hopefully couples will begin to open up and be freer with each other as soon as possible. Those who don't could find the sudden shift too traumatic when the time arrives.

What are some of the things we want to bring out of hiding and expose to the sunshine? There are several which seem particularly significant. We need to willingly let them be seen.

1. *Let our love be seen.*

For decades our spouse has seen sacrificial evidences of our love toward our children. Too often it came at the expense of our couple-love. Love must now escape from the shadows and come into full view.

"Better is open rebuke than hidden love" (Proverbs 27:5).

Hidden love is one of the cruelest forms of love. Hidden love remains a mystery. No one should have to hire a detective to find out if his spouse loves him. No married person should have to pick petals and say, "He loves me, he loves me not."

In word and action each of us will need to express exactly how we feel and leave the guessing game behind.

The sad fact is that if we have not practiced saying the magic words, we will have to work hard to say them now. But it can be done.

2. *Discuss our plans for the future.*

It's time to become serious about the last third of our lives. If God gives us the time together, how are we going to use it? Previously our children may have dictated our agenda, but now we must look reality in the eye and ask where to go from here.

Parents who have graduated from parenting know life will not last forever. What will your next move be? Where will you live? Is there some special place you want to settle? Will you travel? How will it be financed? Will you get a part-time job? What kind of ministry are you interested in?

Most of my friends are in the middle of these kinds of discussions.

Recently a couple stopped in to see us; we had known them for years. They have moved south and love it. They have become involved in community and church activities and are totally satisfied.

We know another couple who have been anxious to move for years. When their last child moved out, they were going to leave the next day for anywhere. But now that the last child is gone, they have decided to stay because both of their children live in the area and they are in no hurry to go anywhere.

Decisions have to be made. Agreements have to be reached. The time has come to discuss plans while remaining flexible enough so God can have final control over all the blueprints.

"Many are the plans in a man's heart, but it is the LORD's purpose that prevails" (Proverbs 19:21).

3. *Create healing.*

If a couple has raised children, paid most of a mortgage, cared for their aging parents, switched jobs a few times, and suffered from hemorrhoids, they need to be healed. Even the best parents may feel that they have been through the proverbial wringer. Going through a wringer has to be a flattening experience.

Most of us remember being overly tired, frustrated, broke, bewildered, and sometimes terribly disappointed with each other. Now the time has come to sit, to touch, to hold, to walk, to listen. Time to feel whole with each other again.

If your partner is no longer around, it's time to feel whole for yourself again.

Often parents feel like enjoying each other's presence as they have not been able to for years. It's a good time. One day at a time for as many days as God will give us.

"A time to heal" (Ecclesiastes 3:3).

4. *Get to know each other again!*

Our spouses aren't the twenty-two-year-old, sprite, wide-eyed youths they once were, but in many ways they still are. Every time I look at my wife I see two women wrapped into one. There is the mature, handsome mother of three grown children who remains the sparkly-eyed cute kid with a grin that still melts me down to my socks.

When the two of us are alone we start to see that young side again. We see the reason why we fell in love and ran pell-mell into marriage.

It's still there. For those who will look again at each other, it's still alive. We got to know our partner first without the children. Now we can get acquainted all over again.

Read the Song of Solomon as if you had never read it before. Apply it not to young people who are lovestruck for the first time. Apply it to a couple who are more seasoned by life experience.

My lover spoke and said to me,
Arise my darling,

my beautiful one, and come with me.
See! The winter is past;
the rains are over and gone.
Flowers appear on the earth;
the season of singing has come,
the cooing of doves
is heard in our land.
The fig tree forms its early fruit;
the blossoming vines spread their fragrance.
Arise, come, my darling;
my beautiful one, come with me (2:10–13).

Now that the "winter has past" and we are alone, we need to notice each other anew. Don't try to make up for lost time. Don't try to recreate yesterday. Neither is possible. Yesterday is gone.

Rather ask where you want to be with each other today. God doesn't make yesterdays. God doesn't promise tomorrows. Today is the only time to become reacquainted.

The Rubber-Band Children

A father told me with a puzzled look, "When I left the house this morning for work, I said goodbye to my twenty-one-year-old son who was sitting on the floor, without shoes, watching cartoons. In my wildest dream I never imagined that this would happen to my family."

He said he would never again say, "That will never happen to me" because the very thing which you are so emphatic about will almost certainly come to pass. It must be a law of physics.

The fact is that millions of adult children return home every year. Often they move back home for reasons we would never have predicted. Children return home because they are lonely, broke, broken-hearted, divorced, pregnant, burned-out, bewildered or because they flunked school. Some come because of unfinished business. Without knowing it, they are trying to establish a bond with their parents which has always eluded them. They want to reach out one more time and feel accepted.

A large part of the flight back to the nest is because of financial pressures. There are also many underlying currents which should not be missed. Often the causes are family, love, psychological, and spiritual. Adult children need a roof on a rainy day but they also may be looking for someone to touch their souls.

Like rubber bands, they stretch out. Some stretch far and some stretch for a long time. But one day they let go; they make a phone call and the rubber band snaps back.

Not every cause is noble

Before we canonize every adult child, we need to say that some come home for terrible reasons. Some are lazy, afraid to take responsibility, refusing to grow up, and avoiding reality. It would be a mistake to treat every child as a wounded, recovering, sensitive puppy. Some don't want to become adults.

A son explained to his father that he didn't want to accept responsibility. If he moved out of the house he would have to make decisions, pay his bills on time, fix his meals, and do his own laundry.

"So," his father concluded, "you want us to carry all your burdens so you won't have to face life. I'm supposed to handle everything because you don't care to."

This son would probably benefit from large amounts of fresh air. That fresh air can best be found outside of his parents' home. Mom or Dad may need to tell him the time-honored quip, "Thirty days hath September, April, June, November, and you."

It isn't always smart to furnish a hide-out for people who refuse to take care of themselves. While Mom and

Dad want to be caring and loving, too much of either under the wrong circumstances will do serious harm to our children.

The adult children we can help

Each family must respond to its own situation. There are no airtight rules that tell us whether or not grown children should return home for an extended period of time. Our own children have moved back from time to time and we were quite pleased about it. Much more than we expected.

Before a rubber-band child returns, discuss the following questions.

1. *Will this hurt or help him?*

Specifically what is there about "home" that will prove beneficial? Does he need time-out, closeness, financial relief, emotional support? What are the healing elements that will be operating?

On the other hand, has the child proven to be irresponsible, and is he moving in to continue avoiding responsibility?

2. *Will this help or hurt the parents?*

The presence of grown children can be a tonic, but there also could be a price to pay. Can you afford to take this step? Will it drive a wedge between the parents? Will the child's presence renew old tensions? Can one parent handle this but not the other one?

3. *Will this force you to go back to parenting?*

Can the young person reenter the home as an adult? Will everyone regress? Will the parents begin telling their twenty-two-year-old how to live? If they can't live together on a fairly equal footing, the process can be painful.

4. *Are there house rules?*

Find out what is important and express it. Will there be alcohol in the house? Can they have boyfriends or girlfriends over? How late is too late to be out, or are there no restrictions? What about meals? Do they have to report for all meals or let someone know, or what?

Do they have to pitch in and help around the house? What is expected of them?

5. *Can you communicate, communicate, communicate?*

If you have had trouble talking in the past, are you prepared to work on it for the future? Everyone is older now and hopefully more mature. Promise that you will force yourself to say how you feel.

A dad told me, "When my kids were growing up, I used to tell myself, 'If my girl ever gets pregnant, she better not come home whining to me. It's her problem and she had better take care of it.' Now I know better. When my kids are really hurting, I want to be there to do what I can. I would help a stranger; why wouldn't I help my own child?"

Some facts to consider

The Bible shines a great deal of light on how we should treat people who are in need. Take those values and apply them to your grown children.

1. *The father who took him back.*

As we have in so many other cases, we look again to the father of the prodigal son. He is a clear and practical example of how a loving parent should act.

After his son had left to live an immoral lifestyle, the father, without hesitation, took him back. Not only did he take him back, but it was with uninhibited enthusiasm.

Because our circumstances may be different, certainly not every parent should do this. But it's all right to be overjoyed if your child is coming home.

"So he got up and went to his father.

But while he was still a long way off, his father saw him and was filled with compassion for him; he ran to his son, threw his arms around him and kissed him" (Luke 15:20).

2. *Do not promote irresponsibility.*

If it is readily evident that our adult child has simply become too lazy to work, we do him a disservice by giving him a place to stay. We help no one by furnishing a haven so he can loaf. In our early years we too may have tried to avoid growing up.

"For even when we were with you, we gave you this rule: 'If a man will not work, he shall not eat' " (2 Thessalonians 3:10).

This serves as a good boundary to protect parents from becoming overprotective and actually hurting everyone involved.

3. *Healing broken hearts.*

As long as people are involved with people, hearts will be broken. We will be wounded, disillusioned, and saddened. Our children will suffer shattering setbacks and sometimes they need a place where they can be made whole again.

When parents are part of the healing process, they do the work of God. God wants to make our spirits and souls healthy. Sometimes He uses parents as special agents who minister to young adults.

"He heals the brokenhearted and binds up their wounds" (Psalm 147:3).

I know parents who let their children move back home because:
- They broke off an engagement and needed to refocus.
- They had an alcohol problem and needed a steady routine.
- They had flunked out of college and needed to regroup.
- They were pregnant and unmarried.
- They had been married to an abuser and became pregnant.

Fortunately these parents were able to be part of a healing ministry to their grown children.

"It was one of the greatest times of my life," a mother explained. "For ten months I drew closer to my daughter than we had ever been. By the time she moved out again, she was in a better spiritual state and so was I."

Those who accept it as a spiritual ministry may find it extremely satisfying. They realize their children need a warm bed, a good meal, and a roof, but they need much more. Those who are able to grow in Christ and see the Holy Spirit work between them are the real beneficiaries.

The psalmist says he wanted to take shelter in the wings of God (61:4). Sometimes we supply a similar place for the people we love. Our home serves as a shelter for a weekend, a month, maybe a year. It's a safe place for someone whose nerves are shattered, whose dreams are muddied, and whose spirit is weak.

If we furnish a shelter for a while, we may have rescued a soul that wasn't sure where to turn next. In this case that soul was our own child.

Sucking Thumbs for Attention

Every day Martha waited by the phone expecting her son, Steve, to call. The two would talk for ten or fifteen minutes and afterwards Martha felt terrific. Her skies were bluer, the flowers smelled sweeter, and the birds sang brightly.

But what if son Steve failed to call? Then Martha sank into a dismal blue funk and remained there all day and well into the evening.

Martha, like many other parents, has connected her happiness and well-being directly to her son, Steve. Mom's attitude leaves it squarely on his shoulders to determine how her day is going to go.

Too many of us have hitched our emotional boxcar to someone else's train. If that person comes through, we chug along well. But when their engine fails to gather steam, we sit all alone on the tracks of life.

The people most likely to depend on their children for emotional energy are the ones who lean heavily on their children. Mothers who were emotionally dependent on their husbands are prime candidates. Men who constantly sought approval from others are also apt to seek almost daily reinforcement from their children.

Moderate reinforcement makes sense. Most of us need people. But emotional dependence on our children is unreasonable.

Going to extremes

Theresa was a prime example of an emotional-dependent. Constantly afraid that her daughter Angela would distance herself, Theresa concentrated on ailments and need for attention. Whenever Angela called or visited, Theresa repeated her litany of complaints:

"I asked the doctor to increase my dosage."

"When I forget to take my medicine, I get dizzy."

"I'm afraid to lift anything."

"My feet hurt when I walk too much."

"If I watch TV my eyes hurt."

And the list goes on. If that seems normal and perfectly acceptable to the reader, this chapter is written for you. This conversation, if it is an average one, is a relationship wrecker. Designed to hold the listener close, it will usually drive the person away. Let's look at what is going on in this relationship.

It's negative.

The conversation centers on what is going wrong. There are times to discuss what isn't working, but not continuously. It is hard to call or visit someone who drones on about negatives.

It's a call for attention.

"Look how bad things are for me" is self-centered and destructive. No relationship can remain healthy if it focuses on one individual and his problems. Even a family relationship will have trouble weathering those storms.

It's an emotional noose.

The parent who does this is trying to tie a rope around someone's neck and hold him close. In many cases this is effective. It may keep the child committed but frequently will result in bitterness and resentment.

Adult children often catch on even if the parent doesn't. Sometimes the parent ties the noose out of habit without giving it a second thought. But when the child figures it out, he becomes angry over this form of emotional abuse.

It's a lack of joy.

We all know someone who has tremendous stress in his life and yet he remains pleasant to be around. His health has hit a bump in the road, he owes too much money, and his dog is slowing down. But despite his problems, he has a great joy, optimism, and playfulness about him. After we spend time with him, we walk away pumped up and eager to return.

Joy is attractive. Joy is magnetic. Joy is contagious. Joy is far more fetching than thumb-sucking.

Parents who depress

I wish I had five dollars for every adult child who told me they hate to visit, call, or read the mail from one or both of their parents. And the parent doesn't have to be old to fall into the monster category.

Dan from Ohio said,

"Every time I go to see my dad, he tells me what a failure he has been. His job has turned to dust and he has practically no pension plan waiting. I don't mind hearing about his problems, but just once in a while would be plenty. With him it's every time."

Eileen from Nebraska said,

"Mom wants me to move closer to her. She thinks that since I'm divorced I have no ties anyway. What she really wants is for me to keep her company. I can't spend the rest of my life keeping her company."

Linda from Indiana had a different wrinkle,

"With us it's my brother. He can't hold a job or do anything right. Never could. Whenever I call or go see my mother we seem to hold a wake for dear old brother.

" 'Ain't it awful.' 'He never writes.' 'He doesn't do this and doesn't do that.' A little bit of that goes a long way. I wish we were baseball fans so we had something else to talk about."

Most of us have relatives that we can "feel" when they come into a room. Our stomachs go into knots. Our anxiety level leaps. It might be an obnoxious cousin or a teasing uncle.

These situations are bad enough. But when parents send their grown children into panic attacks, life really gets difficult. None of us can afford to send our children into emotional trauma.

Emotional blackmail

Not many of us would intentionally plot and scheme to hold on to our children. But many of us may do it unconsciously. Look at the following list and see if you use similar phrases. They may carry messages with powerful enslaving force.

• Oh, don't worry about me; I'm just an old person, not good for much.

• So you finally found time to call!

• I almost died when you were born.

• Oh, no. Go skiing for the holidays! I guess I'll just watch Andy Williams specials.

• It cost a lot of money to send you to tech school.

• You don't want seconds on the sweet potatoes? I burned my hand taking them out of the microwave.

• Your brother Lance never comes to visit.

• Did I tell you I almost died when you were born?

• I don't know why, but Thanksgiving is always sad for me.

• I understand. Everybody's busy. It's hard to fit your parents in.

• You're going to the Grand Canyon instead of coming to see us?

• Friday we're going to preplan our funerals. I thought you might want to be there.

• I just thought you might want to sit with us in church on Reformation Sunday. It means so much to your grandmother.

• By the way, did I ever mention that I almost died when you were born?

Emotional blackmail is a highly personalized art form. What works for one parent may fail for another. These may not be the exact words we use, but the ideas are there.

Most often emotional blackmail works on some-one's weakness. Where is the adult child soft or tender? Sometimes the parent uses his weakness ("I don't mind being alone") or the parent uses his strength ("I've been thinking about getting rid of my power tools. If you hap-pen to drop by this weekend, we could talk about it").

Frankly, emotional blackmail is cruel. I knew a wom-an who gave each of her grown children several thousand dollars a year—if they were deserving. What did deserv-ing mean? They had to be available when she wanted them. If they failed to respond on time or in a proper man-ner, she simply reduced the stipends. When they were particularly naughty she cut it out altogether that year.

The process worked. Each of them returned to rest under her wings and regain her financial blessing. But at what cost?

Take inventory

What system have you drifted into? What emotion-al tether have you tied around your children? Look for pet phrases you use when you want them to do some-thing. Some are overt forms of verbal torture. They are designed to get the victim to give in (e.g., the mother with the money). Others are nasty habits we slide into without realizing it ("Oh, you go without me; I don't feel well anyway").

If we want to improve relationships, we have to eliminate emotional blackmail. Ask your spouse or ask a friend if they see manipulation in your phrases, your voice tone, your offers and deals. They may be able to see some twists that you cannot see.

From time to time say to yourself:

• If I have to pout to get them to visit, I don't want them to come.

• When I invite them to visit, I will emphasize the positive reasons and not lean on the negative.

• I will not weave webs designed to trap my children into doing things they don't want to do.

• I pledge never to exaggerate my aches, pains, or other ailments simply to get their attention.

Checks and balances

Whenever we wonder whether we are pouting just to manipulate our children, we can look to the Bible for help. The Scriptures keep us from going to extremes. Double-check these attitudes. Look at a few great verses in Proverbs 15.

1. *Be open and honest.*

Deceit is always a lousy way to deal with relatives. It may be good in warfare, chess, and magic, but deceit only hurts relationships.

When adult children discover that you tricked them into calling or coming over, they will resent it and they will be cautious the next time. Christians, no matter how lonely, need to live on a higher plane than this.

"The tongue that brings healing is a tree of life, but a deceitful tongue crushes the spirit" (Proverbs 15:4).

There's nothing wrong with inviting our relatives over but we have to be honest about it. (One of the rare exceptions is to trick someone into attending his surprise birthday party. That's still living on a high plain.)

2. *Cheerfulness is attractive.*

Do you remember when your children were little whiners? You can recall the first-class headache their behavior gave you.

Cheerfulness draws people faster than a fire sale. It's fun to be around people who enjoy life. The Lord can help us enjoy being here and consequently people will enjoy being around us.

"The cheerful heart has a continual feast" (Proverbs 15:15).

We are more fun to be around when we see life as a banquet prepared by God.

3. *People love good news.*

Lord, protect us from a long afternoon of "Boy, ain't it awful." None of us has to live in the Valley of Complaints. There are a few things worth grousing about, but we can quickly let it get out of hand.

What if we called our relatives and asked, "How would you like to come over for a cup of coffee and three or four hours of complaining?" They aren't likely to hop on the freeway and speed right over.

The Bible reminds us how much people love good news. Not necessarily big news or startling news, simply good news.

"Good news gives health to the bones" (Proverbs 15:30).

Imagine our adult children saying to their spouses, "Let's hustle over to see Mom and Dad. We could get all charged up."

If that doesn't sound likely, it is nevertheless possible. Many parents are a pleasure to be around.

A Mother-in-Law
Is No Joke

If you want to get a cheap laugh from an audience, simply say the word "mother-in-law." Your listeners will raise their ears in anticipation and grins will sweep across their faces. They know what they are about to hear will be funny.

Like lawyer jokes or coach jokes or PMS jokes, mother-in-laws have become tantalizing subjects. The very thought of them brings us to an emotional high. As with most humor, it is the mixture of pain and pleasure, the blend of truth and fiction, the experience of frustration and satisfaction which makes them easy victims of laughter.

The fact is that a mother-in-law is a very important person. As a mother she has played a significant role in making her children who they are. The irony is that since a mother-in-law's role is not clearly defined, she can be a loose cannon rolling across the deck of someone else's life.

Most mothers-in-law are unsure of their status. In their attempt to discover their place in this new relationship they become the unfortunate objects of comedy. They aren't sure when to speak up, when to shut up, when to stand up or when to give up. A mother-in-law could learn how to do most of this; but sadly by the time some have learned, they have made many mistakes.

That's why it is important to learn mother-in-law-ing. It is just as important to become educated in daughter-in-lawing and son-in-lawing. These are unnatural relationships. They are unlikely to simply fall into place comfortably. But because there are so many good stories, we know the relationship can be enjoyable and rewarding.

Sitting on the fence

Picture a mother-in-law sitting on the fence of life. On one side of the fence is a good relationship. On the other side lies strain and resistance. Mother-in-law has the potential of falling on either side. Which way will the wind blow and where will she land?

We continuously meet both kinds. A woman called in during a talk show we were on and said, "I'm not calling for advice. I've already filed for divorce. But I want to let you know that my mother-in-law made my life miserable.

"Before I got married my husband looked like the devoted son, thoughtful of his aging mother. Soon afterwards I discovered he was a hopeless slave to anything she said or asked."

At the same time we remember so many adults saying things like, "Oh, I get along great with his mother. Even after we divorced I remained friends with her."

Mothers-in-law are neither inherently good nor inherently evil. They can fall either way. That has always been true. However, today, because of so many divorces, that good mother-in-law can also climb back up on the fence and fall down on the bad side. Changing times and changing relationships can make monsters of us all.

A wounded mother-in-law

One of nature's most dangerous creatures is an injured mother-in-law. There is no telling what or when she will charge. Her potential to inflict damage is considerable. A smart spouse doesn't try to stand between a mother and her child, even if that child is forty-five years old.

When a mother-in-law feels she has been slighted, insulted, or abused, she could turn with little warning. It is important to keep our balance and not become sensitive or easily offended.

A mother-in-law at war can make life miserable. A good woman keeps her cool, holds her opinions, and shares her love.

A hot button

Of all the subjects we have discussed in small groups and at seminars, none causes as much uproar as mother-in-law. Shy people speak up immediately. Bored people perk up and pay attention. Placid people become emotionally involved in the discussion. Opinions, experiences, and feelings fly across the room.

What do we do if we are on a radio call-in show and everything turns quiet? Simply mention the word mother-in-law and the phone lines light up. As you read this chapter, doubtless your mind is racing in several directions as you think about your situation and how it operates.

Some surveys indicate that fifty percent of the population enjoy their mothers-in-law while the other half are driven to distraction. That's the good news and the bad news. The relationship is packed with potential. Smart people learn to harness this energy constructively while others let it turn into a volcano of devastating proportions.

Change is tough

When children get married, the relationship with their parents changes immediately and drastically. Since most change is difficult, this one can be especially rough. Mother has been a major factor in nurturing her child for years. Now, suddenly, abruptly, another person enters her child's life and takes over the main role. What is she supposed to do? Is she expected to turn off her brooding, protective instincts simply because a minister made a pronouncement and everyone tossed rice? That's asking a great deal. No wonder many mothers find it a tricky transition to make. Surely they can be forgiven if they act awkwardly at first and make a few mistakes.

The mothers-in-law who create the most havoc are the ones who don't want to change. They want to keep their mothering role and in some cases even extend it to the new child-in-law. Afraid of losing their identity and purpose, they cling as if they still have ducklings to fuss over.

At the same time we can hear many mothers-in-law protesting that the problem is two-sided. Her married children frequently want her around as a baby-sitter, as a financier, as a painter, as a chauffeur, but not as a person. Too often mothers-in-law see their grown children as inconsiderate, selfish complainers who treat them as little more than convenience stores.

Social change, too

The normal transitions in an extended family are enough to produce tension. It has always been so. Farm families in tightly knit communities have problems defining everyone's role almost as much as urban and suburban families do. The creation of new families is hard in and of itself.

Today that transition is made all the more difficult by the rapid changes in our society. Divorce, mobility, remarriage, and stepfamilies make the mother-in-law situation more complex. Whose mother-in-law is she, anyway? Whose grandmother is she? How will she know when to help, when to back off, and when to ignore the situation?

Despite all the social upheaval, it is still possible to be a level-headed mother-in-law. Millions have learned to play a balanced role. They are accepted, loved, admired, and cherished. At every discussion of mothers-in-law a number of people will raise their hands and say, "I don't know what you are talking about; I have the greatest mother-in-law in the world." Or they will say, "I get along better with my mother-in-law than I do with my spouse."

Half of the mothers-in-law seem to be doing it correctly, even in a rapidly changing world. The other half, who are getting bad reviews, could learn more about the ingredients that go into a fine relationship. Unfortunately some have pretty shabby sons-in-law and daughters-in-law, and the job can be tough.

Spiritual dimensions

The Bible offers us great guidelines, none better than the example of Naomi in the book of Ruth. It is a terrific text on how to be a releasing mother-in-law.

We also need to consider the spiritual applications of acceptance, forgiveness, freedom, maturity, love, and growth. How do individuals "leave and cleave" without dumping the relationships with their parents which they once held so closely? What kind of interaction did the apostle Peter have with his mother-in-law (Matthew 8:14; Luke 4:38)?

A spiritual life draws on the qualities which make people worth knowing. Spirituality, in the Christian sense, reduces our jealousy, our vengefulness, our anger, our touchiness, our fear and insecurity, our greed, and much more. Though we may struggle with an uneasy relationship, we gain a better sense of balance when we sift it through our spiritual reality. Hopefully this book will call us in that direction.

The happy prospect

Two types of people need to learn mother-in-lawing: those who are mothers-in-law and those who have mothers-in-law. There are certain patterns which are destructive. Some of us are trapped in them. There are other behaviors which can help us get along not only well but even constructively. Behavior patterns can be learned, nurtured, and perfected.

A woman told us that she had worked out an excellent understanding with her mother-in-law. When she visited the elderly woman's home she simply did everything her mother-in-law's way. Then when her mother-in-law visited this woman's home, they did everything her mother-in-law's way. This pattern seemed to work best for their survival.

Mother-in-lawing doesn't have to be a foxhole experience. The relationship needs to be thought through carefully and handled deliberately. In-laws can get along well if there is mutual respect and cheerfulness.

Spiritual patterns

Let's look to the Bible for guidelines. How can a mother-in-law know how to help without interfering? Consider some of these spiritual and yet practical lessons.

1. *Don't visit too often.*

I knew a mother-in-law who lived next door to her children and she "bounced in" whenever she felt like it. She didn't knock. She simply bounced in at any hour.

The Bible teaches us to measure how often we go to a neighbor's house. We can wear out our welcome. Let our children learn to miss us just a little.

"Seldom set foot in your neighbor's house—too much of you, and he will hate you" (Proverbs 25:17).

2. *Learn tongue biting.*

Good mothers-in-law as well as fathers-in-law have black and blue tongues. They got those from watching their grandchildren. Whenever their children disciplined the grandchildren too much or too little, the grandparents chomped down on their own tongues.

Grandmother wants to say something. She is dying to say something. But she knows it will only hurt everyone.

At a social not long ago a young grandfather was asked how he liked grandfathering. He replied, "Oh, he's a great little kid," and then he whispered, "but he'd be a lot better if I could straighten him out without his parents around."

The best in-laws eat a steady diet of tongue. They learn not to be busybodies and not to gossip or spread verbal destruction.

"Besides, they get into the habit of being idle and going about from house to house. And not only do they become idlers, but also gossips and busybodies, saying things they ought not to" (1 Timothy 5:13).

3. *They speak with healing words.*

A mother-in-law can still have a beneficial, uplifting role in her grown child's life if she is willing to say helpful things. Helpful comments, however, are not easy if we have a habit of critical, demanding, and negative conversation.

We need to praise our adult children for:

    Their selection of a mate.

    Their choice of wallpaper.

    Their career and job choices.

    Their choice of a church or small group.

Most young adults do not prosper from their mother-in-law's hurtful statements. They do, however, flourish from a continuous and sincere spray of compliments, praise, and encouragement. Every mother-in-law does well to ask herself what the tenor of her conversation is.

"Pleasant words are a honeycomb, sweet to the soul and healing to the bones" (Proverbs 16:24).

4. *Show respect for their individuality.*

"Those kids have an awful lot to learn about life," said a mother-in-law. "Why we're over at their place half the time trying to straighten out their mess."

She was talking about a couple in their middle-thirties who had been married for six or seven years. Unfortunately she saw her calling in life to rescue these young people from themselves.

By butting in uninvited, this woman demonstrated a great lack of respect for the couple. A large part of respect means we are free to make our own mistakes. Good parents let their little children and their grown children make their own mistakes.

The biblical principle states it this way: "Show proper respect to everyone" (1 Peter 2:17).

When we interfere, when we intrude, when we take over, we run roughshod over someone else's dignity. Everyone needs the privilege of making his own mistakes.

Another parent said, "We messed up plenty when we were starting out. We don't want to see that happen to our kids."

Far better that they burn every meal, wreck their car radiator, overdraft checks, fail to pay their taxes, lose their house keys . . . far better all of this and more than for a parent to take over and puncture the child's self-respect.

What about fathers-in-law?

Frankly, from all of our research and all of our interviews, we have found very little trouble coming from the dad side. It does happen, but most of the friction comes if the son or son-in-law works for Dad. Otherwise Dad is not typically in the nurturing business.

Naturally the same rules and guidelines apply to him as to her, but he seems to sense that. In most cases he has far less interest in fixing people. We have tried extensively to dig up complaints about fathers and their grown children. They do exist but they are very rare.

What Are We Afraid Of?

People of all ages suffer from it. It is a child's number one fear and the same is true of Grandma. We are afraid we are going to be abandoned and left alone. Children worry what will happen to them if their parents don't come back. They hear about murders and divorces and death and they know it could affect their parents.

Adults have the same apprehension. Most of us were not created to live alone. While some flourish that way, the majority don't. We know a lot of people but we bond with ten or fewer. A few family members and a handful of friends will just about cover it in most cases.

Three of the people we bonded with were our children. Even if we disagreed, fought, and aggravated each other, we still hoped there was something special, something lifelong, between us. Now time, marriage, careers, geography, and circumstances could pry us apart.

Will these changes create emotional differences as well as geographical? Are we losing something that will leave a large and painful gap in our lives? Our adult children face the same uncertainty as they leave to take on an unpredictable world.

Trying to adjust

You can see it in the eyes of people our age. Many are restless, even fidgety. Their last child has packed and moved out. Now they are looking around, like a cat on a roof trying to figure out how to jump.

"We just decided to change everything. Donald took a job in Denver and the two of us moved out there. I never thought we would do that at fifty, but away we went. Looking back now, I think we simply didn't know how to deal with our loss. Donald thought we should do something. Do anything."

Five years later Donald and Marie were as confused as ever. They were still uneasy and had trouble re-establishing themselves. Neither of them could cope with the empty feelings they had inside.

"We looked around," another woman explained. "Even took a few trips to Florida and Georgia, house hunting. I can't say what we were looking for, but we felt unsettled. Finally we decided that new scenery wasn't the answer for us, so we stayed where we were."

Why does our anxiety level increase?

Most people describe these as happy times after the children leave, but not everyone does. About 40 percent contact a divorce lawyer soon after the last child moves out. Most parents report an increase in their anxiety level.

What causes that increase? First, let's define anxiety for the purpose of this discussion.

Fear has an object. I am afraid of dogs, airplanes, burglars, or whatever. There is a reason why I am afraid. Fear has a real basis.

Anxiety is a ghost. It means I am nervous about something I can't see and can only poorly define. We may be anxious about life. Anxiety suggests there is something lurking. Something might happen but we aren't sure what.

Fears are much easier to deal with than anxiety. If you are afraid because of a noise in your car engine, you can get that checked. But if cars make you anxious, that's harder to fix. Apprehension is the mild case; anxiety might give you ulcers.

Let's look at a few of the leading causes of anxiety regarding grown children.

1. *Our lack of involvement.*

Mrs. Penderson is anxious if the telephone rings or if the telephone doesn't ring. If it rings she knows something has happened to one of the kids. When it doesn't ring she is just as certain that something happened and they don't want to call her. The bottom line is that Mrs. Penderson believes something bad is always about to happen to one of her children.

In her case, absence makes the heart grow shaky. When the children were home she could watch over them rather carefully. She always looked after their needs, hovered just a little, and doted quite a bit. If they were in trouble, Mom got involved, did something about it, and fixed it. Miles away they can no longer bring it to Mom, cry on her shoulder, or ask her to mend it.

The fears drop but the anxieties increase. Still hoping to keep them from pain, she worries about how they are doing.

"We don't stop worrying," one mother explained. "No matter how old they get, you still wonder what's happening to them."

2. *Too much free time.*

If we fail to fill up our lives with other ventures, we are bound to worry about something. Idle minds are almost certain to become negative and overwrought. How many of us with nothing to do in the evenings will begin to fret? It doesn't take long for an empty head to imagine all sorts of ghosts and goblins.

The number one thing that adult children want us to tell their parents is G.A.L.—Get A Life. The lack of constructive endeavors degenerates into too much concern for our children.

A serious gap has been left by our children and it is our responsibility to fill that space; it is not their responsibility. Read that again.

3. *Our failure to grow.*

Anyone who fights to hold on to the past has trouble accepting the present. Today could become the most satisfying, fulfilling time of our lives. Our unwillingness to seize the moment leaves us suspended in the past.

Many of us have to change our attitudes about today. This can be the most exciting time of our lives. If we don't believe that, then we will become fixed on the past and continue to be anxious over our children.

The author of Proverbs uses a phrase that could serve us well. "I was filled with delight day after day"

(8:30). Anxiety will steal all the delight from the present.

Anxiety and spiritual growth

A twenty-five-year-old daughter is going to drive to New Orleans with a friend. The trip will take her eight hours. Many parents will tell their adult child, "Be sure to call when you get there so I'll know you're safe."

According to our definition of fear, you have almost nothing to be afraid of. People drive those distances every day without mishap or mayhem. The odds are a million to one that anything seriously wrong will happen to them. Something terrible could occur, but the chances are almost infinitesimal.

But the very thought of anything happening to grown children sends some parents into anxiety attacks. It is the thought that bothers them, and not the facts.

One middle-aged couple told us anxiety now works in reverse. When they go someplace, their child tells them to be careful and to call when they get home. They are suffering from a type of genetic reversal.

Spiritual growth could help deliver us from anxiety overload. The ghosts of anxiety can frequently be chased back into the closet by spiritual exercise. There are some basic steps.

1. *Identify what is going on.*

Fretting over our grown son's final exams in far off Seattle is irrational. We could stay up all night, walk the floor, make hot coffee, and eat brownies, but none of that will help. In fact, our continued anxiety will only hurt us in the long run.

The writer of Proverbs recognized the problem three thousand years ago. Anxiety didn't arrive with the computer age.

"An anxious heart weighs a man down" (Proverbs 12:25).

It's destructive. It's a killer. It even wrecks our relationships with our children. Admit what is going on and we have taken the first step in spiritual growth.

2. *Aim for an anxiety-free relationship.*

Since anxiety is destructive, it can't be helpful. If we worry because our son is about to buy a used car in Pittsburgh, we haven't accomplished anything. If we call and pester him about his down payment or warn him against getting a convertible, we only drive a wedge.

The Bible tells us this as a simple truth.

"Do not be anxious about anything" (Philippians 4:6).

Action may help, but fretting never does. Look at what Jesus Christ taught us.

"Who of you by worrying can add a single hour to his life?" (Matthew 6:27).

Worrying doesn't work. All of us know that, but it doesn't stop us. Knocking on wood doesn't give us good luck, throwing salt over our shoulder is useless, and crossing our fingers is dumb. But some of us do those, too.

Continued worry will likely hurt everyone. Say that to yourself slowly.

3. *Put your anxiety in God's lap.*

Tell the Lord something like this: "Lord, I can't fly the plane that Peggy is on. I certainly can't land it. I can't even serve her lunch. Consequently, I'm going to give the trip, the plane, Peggy, and the luggage all to you. Give me the peace that you will be there the entire time."

Having said that in faith, go and find something else to do. You have exercised your spiritual commitment.

"Cast all your anxiety on him" (1 Peter 5:7).

For some of us it isn't easy. We have to hand the deal to God and an hour later hand it to Him again and an hour later. . . . But with practice we get better. We have been programmed to carry our own burdens around. It may take time to reprogram.

4. *Expect God to give us peace.*

That's what faith is. If we give something to God and ask Him to handle it, we have to believe He will. To take something to God and think, "I know it won't make any difference anyway," isn't faith that moves mountains.

The psalmist had a great experience releasing his anxiety to God. It could be our experience, too.

"When anxiety was great within me, your consolation brought joy to my soul" (Psalm 94:19).

Consolation and joy like that might take practice on our part, but it is available. Spiritual experiences are not the same as religious meetings. Spiritual growth comes from putting our anxieties into God's lap and leaving them there.

In his excellent book about finding meaning in life,[1] Dr. Paul Welter reminds us of this pivotal point. We need to take our focus off the object of our anxiety and look up to God. Depression makes us look down, but gratitude causes us to look up and fills us with praise.

The Philippians 4:6 and 7 passage we referred to seems important in our spiritual freedom. The apostle Paul doesn't tell us to simply stop concentrating on our anxieties. He tells us to let our requests be made known unto God with an attitude of gratitude. As a result of thankful prayerfulness we find the peace of God.

A new commitment

When our children were babies, many of us either had them baptized or dedicated to the Lord. Those of us who did not dedicate them in church probably dedicated them at home or within our own hearts.

Maybe we need to consider a second dedication: the dedication of our grown children. In some meaningful moment, not quickly or lightly, we should consider committing our adult children into the hands of God. We could tell the Lord that we can't hold them in our hands anymore, but we know that God can.

Our traditional rites of passage have become blurred. When does a child become an adult child? Are

---

1. Paul Welter, *Counseling and the Search for Meaning,* 99.

they really our children all of our lives? Maybe we need to prayerfully declare their independence. We need to let go of our worries about their next trip to Boston and all the other symbolic trips thereafter.

Regrets? We Have a Few

Her name was Margaret and she had moved to the United States from Germany. A widow for over twenty years, this spunky woman with a thick accent lived in a mobile home with her forty-year-old son, Frederick.

Margaret was a terrific Christian woman with a ready smile and a quick wit. Despite some obvious hardships, she lived in fellowship with the Lord and was eager to share her faith.

In one of her more somber moments this picture of courage let down her guard and asked me the question that really haunted her.

"I raised Frederick in a Christian home. I took him to Sunday school and church. After his father died I worked twice as hard to be close to him. But despite everything I did, I couldn't stop him from becoming an alcoholic. What in the world did I do wrong?"

That question echoes in the minds of millions of Christian parents. Where did we go wrong? How did we fail? Why didn't our children turn out to be the finished pearls we planned for them to be?

It's popular to blame parents

Parents are quick to blame themselves for all of their children's imperfections. If they have poor posture, lazy work habits, messy rooms, too few friends, too many friends, or they play tuba in a polka band, we think it is our fault. We are gigantic magnets who pull every imaginable guilt toward ourselves.

In most eras parents probably wished they could have done more to help their children, but in the present age guilt has become an agonizing preoccupation. Today's popular attitude suggests that if there is *anything* wrong with us, we can trace the problem directly back to our parents.

Why are our children short or bald? Why can't they sing bass in the church quartet? If it wasn't for halting parents, surely everyone would be Rhodes scholars. Blaming parents has gone to a maddening extreme.

Most of us have some regrets as parents, even if we did our best. But when psychology or counseling or psychics or television talk shows or magazine articles try to blame every wart on parents, we accept the guilt far too readily. By the fact that we become the garbage cans for blame, parents become receptacles for every real and imagined imperfection.

Guilt will continue to be dumped in our laps as long as we are willing to accept it.

Certainly we were far from perfect. Most of us were merely normal or average. But our weaknesses are no reason to accept all of the responsibility for how our children are turning out.

The problem of being guilt-bound

When parents accept the responsibility for *every* blemish in their children's lives, they prevent two good things from happening.

One, we can't deal with our real mistakes because we believe we ruined everything. The fact is, we did things wrong, but we didn't do everything wrong. How do we process our real regrets if we take the blame for everything?

Two, by accepting too much blame we stop our children from accepting responsibility. If we worked hard to make our children into students and they refused, that is not our fault. It is the child's. Grown children will not be able to accept responsibility for their own conduct as long as they are encouraged to blame their parents.

A young man told me he had inadequate parents. They tried tirelessly to make him get better grades. Each evening they sat at the table and went over his work. They grounded him if he did poorly. They followed his every move in an attempt to improve his grades.

"They failed," he insisted smugly. "Despite all they did, my parents couldn't make me get good grades."

Hold on. Did I miss something here? He refused to study. He fought every subject. And it was his parents' fault that he didn't get better grades? Shouldn't the son have been responsible for getting his work done? How did this blame get shifted to his parents?

There is a limit to responsibility

Read carefully the familiar story of Rahab and the spies in the book of Joshua. It gives us a great lesson about individual responsibility.

The Israelites sent two spies to Jericho to check out the enemy in preparation for an invasion. Rahab hid the spies in her home. Before they left to return to the armies of Israel, Rahab made them promise her something. When the soldiers came, they would not harm any member of her family.

Readily the spies agreed. But they had a stipulation. Her family members were to remain in her house during the siege because, as they explained, "If anyone goes outside your house into the street, his blood will be on his own head; we will not be responsible" (Joshua 2:19).

There is a boundary to accountability. At some point the other person has to be responsible for his own actions. The spies could not guarantee the safety of Rahab's family no matter what they did. If they were going to act like fools and wander out into the battle, they were risking their own necks.

Every person must ultimately be responsible for his choices and behavior. With each passing year children must become increasingly accountable. Except in cases of extreme child abuse, each person is capable of deciding what kind of person he wants to become.

The Bible is packed with passages that speak of individual accountability (Hebrews 13:17; 1 Peter 4:5). God is not quick to shift responsibility from child to parent.

It is prejudice to the extreme to believe that all parents are guilty of something.

Did you run off with another man while your teen was in the tenth grade? That's a problem.

Did you go fishing instead of going to your daughter's graduation? That's a problem.

Did you gamble away the mortgage money and have to move your family? That sounds like guilt.

Did you hit your teenager in a fit of anger? You need to deal with that one.

Did you lie to your child? A genuine apology could be in order.

Deal with facts instead of feelings at this point. All of us could have done better. The real question here is what did we do that was wrong.

Ask for forgiveness

Be brave enough to bring up the subject. Confession is a giant step toward healing. Your child may have been confused for years over what happened and why it happened. They need to see an excellent model of a parent who is willing to take the first step toward reconciliation.

What if it doesn't matter? Suppose you have done something wrong and your child doesn't know about it. Should you go and tell him anyway? Imagine that you went to a convention in 1987 and got drunk. Do you need to tell your child that?

Ask yourself these two questions.

One, does it affect your child directly? Maybe there are other people we need to apologize to but not our children.

Two, will it hurt more than help? Does your apology address a need in the child's life, or will the mention of it cause him grief which has no purpose?

Don't be obsessed with confession. Some people seem to think they need to tell everything to everybody. That kind of attitude can do tremendous damage.

Biblical guidelines for dealing with real guilt

Before we rush off to set everything right with our children, go over the following verses. Confession may be different for each of us, but these are boundaries to keep in mind.

1. *Confess what you did wrong.*

The temptation is to say, "I did this wrong, but remember you did plenty wrong, too." Confessing what we did wrong means to confess only what we did and not bring up what they did wrong.

"I confess my iniquity; I am troubled by my sin" (Psalm 38:18).

Confession isn't tit-for-tat. Confession isn't an excuse to dig at the other person. If your kid did you dirty a thousand times, right now you are only dealing with what you did.

2. *Take the initiative.*

Suppose your child is angry because you were never home. Don't wait for him to come to you. Go to him and say you are sorry. Christian confession is aggressive confession. We take the first step.

In the Sermon on the Mount Jesus taught us to take the initiative.

"Therefore, if you are offering your gift at the altar and there remember that your brother has something against you, leave your gift there in front of the altar. First go and be reconciled to your brother; then come and offer your gift" (Matthew 5:23–24).

3. *Tell God what you did wrong.*

Getting along with our family is tightly intertwined with our ability to get along with God. When we make mistakes, do things that are wrong, or deliberately sin, we need to make it square with God, too.

The Scripture encourages us to tell God what we did wrong.

"If we confess our sins, he is faithful and just and will forgive us our sins and purify us from all unrighteousness" (1 John 1:9).

Touch all the bases. Don't leave people out and don't ignore God. Cleansing, freedom, and forgiveness come because we contacted everyone.

4. *Forget it and move on.*

Guilt is of limited value. Guilt makes us face up to what is wrong and it helps us straighten it out. But perpetual, endless guilt isn't helpful to anyone.

The book of Hebrews quotes God saying, "For I will forgive their wickedness and will remember their sins no more" (8:12).

Never stockpile guilt. You will find plenty of new guilt in the days to come. The very heart of the Christian life is forgiveness and freedom. The forgiveness cycle isn't complete if we have not been set free.

Handle it and remember it no more.

Few regrets

As we talked to veteran parents, we were pleased to see how many had only a few regrets. They seemed to recognize and accept their own limitations. Because they were not abusers, they realize that they fit into the circle of "acceptable" parents. If they had it to do over again, most would have followed the same pattern.

Parenting is not a "guilty occupation." It isn't drug dealing or car-jacking. God created parents and most of us do a fairly creditable job.

The Best Years of Our Lives?

"The greatest year of my life was when I was a senior in high school" declared a character on radio. "Boy, did I have it made."

That was a terrific year for many of us. We knew how to run the school, and the administration tolerated us. The teachers didn't want to take any chances that we might flunk and come back another year.

"For me, it was grade school," a woman in her late forties remembered. Grade school was an age of innocence for many. Boys were only a nuisance in those years and the ravages of puberty had yet to set in. Junior high was still lurking around the corner with its vicious attack on our self-worth.

The best years of our lives may be difficult to nail down. But for many graduate parents the latter third of their lives is a candidate for some of the best.

Look at a few of the changes:

- It's easier to find the TV remote.
- If we put our favorite snack in the refrigerator, it's still there in the morning.
- The school principal never calls.
- No one asks us embarrassing questions about calculus.
- When you buy an ice cream cone, you don't have to pay for six of them.
- We can watch a black and white movie without being ridiculed.
- We don't have to stay up until the last kid is in.
- We don't feel guilty spending money on ourselves.
- The cupboard is packed with our favorite kinds of cereal.
- Our weekends are open to chase whatever larks we care to chase.

This is frosting on the cake. The real substance is stacked layer on layer beneath the surface. Millions of us are picking out dreams and chasing rainbows.

Typically, here are some of the reasons why these are among the best years.

1. *Many of us are retiring early.*

The new retiree doesn't become idle. He or she bails out of a regular job around fifty-five or sixty-two and finds something else. This allows him to accomplish two goals:

One, find a part-time job.

Two, concentrate on the thing he always wanted to do.

George took early retirement from an auto firm at half his regular salary. Every summer he goes to Maine and works in the tourist industry. Winters find George back home deeply involved in his church and community. In many ways these are the most satisfying years of his life.

Carol talked to her accountant about retiring at age sixty-two. She decided there was no reason to wait until sixty-five. Today, Carol enjoys writing a column for the local paper and speaking to ladies' groups.

Dan quietly studied and passed his license to drive a truck. Now he's looking for the right time to inform his boss. Grinding gears and hauling goods two or three days a week would help Dan fulfill a lifelong ambition.

Some of the happiest people are those who shift lifestyles instead of quitting altogether. They re-career instead of retire, and they do it early.

2. *We become snowbirds.*

It was always my dream to move. The day our last child graduated from high school I could picture myself driving a moving van out of the driveway. That didn't happen. In fact, I am probably more content to live where I am than ever before.

Instead, I want to become a snowbird. They say snowbirds have the best of both worlds. Traveling on weekends, or for weeks or even months, they then turn around and go home.

This allows them to keep strong ties with family, church, and community. It also opens up parts of the world they always wanted to check out.

Making a total move works for some and not for others. Uprooting is too traumatic for many. Often the husband wants to go and the wife wants to stay. For them snowbirding might be perfect. Those who no longer have spouses (and there are many) have less to consider.

The truth is most of us stay put. We may travel more but only for short jaunts. Despite all of our talk and dreams, many of us never seem to get going.

3. *We exercise more.*

Do you have trouble picturing your grandfather in his basement, walking on a treadmill with his earphones on listening to classical music? Grandfather would have had trouble imagining it, too.

But not the new grandparents. That's exactly what they are doing. The forty-, fifty-, sixty-, seventy-, and eighty-year-old parents are walking, jogging, swimming, golfing, playing tennis, lifting weights, and all other manner of huffing and puffing.

Those who exercise moderately report that they feel spunkier, think clearer, want to do more, and have better attitudes. Many learn good nutrition and take care of their health.

This seems to contribute highly to the feeling that these are great years. Not many people fold up at fifty and dedicate their energies to the rocking chair.

4. *We are discount happy.*

For the next decade or so businesses will continue to center their efforts on attracting graduate parents and their ilk. Not that we are clambering for stores to give us special rates. Rather businesses are literally pushing discounts on the middle-aged.

Restaurants, movies, banks, and motels ask the white-templed, bifocaled group to please accept their reduced prices. As most of us know, we were bombarded by waitresses, clerks, and ticket takers years before we were eligible asking if we were "senior citizens." Let the good times roll. We would never want to discourage businesses from showing the milk of human kindness.

Not long ago I spoke at a carry-in dinner sponsored by a bank for its "club" customers. A couple of hundred people attended with little more in common than their age and free checking. They are happy to have every discount available.

Looking for security or risk?

I asked a group of friends in their fifties if they were more interested in saving for security or taking risks. Their answer was both. They want to winter in Florida and save money at the same time.

Most people want to take measured risks and go for measured security.

"Working for total security can get you a serious illness," John explained. "Why should I work until I drop when I can taper off and get the best out of life?"

"I'm looking for hobby-income," volunteered Ted. "I have all these projects I want to pursue. If I could work twenty hours a week building my own gadgets and selling them, I think I could be real content."

Wouldn't you miss working with others?

"Not really," Linda jumped in. "The people where I work are okay but still it's a hassle. They mess up and it messes you up. Working alone has a lot to offer."

"I'd like to finally work with my sons," Jim added. "They could run the bulk of the business and I could fill in the gaps. That way I could spend a month in Texas and then come back for three or four months. I think I'd enjoy the variety and change of pace."

These weren't conversations with people in their seventies. These men and women are in their fifties. They don't want to keep working until the day they die. Neither do they want to become idle. A little risk. A little security. It seems like the best of both worlds.

People want to be active but they no longer have a great sense of loyalty to the plant, the foundry, or the corporation. There aren't many gold watches to collect after fifty faithful years and even if there are, people don't want to stick around for them.

There is a sense of freedom, prosperity, adventure, and well-being that few other generations have known. They know the next generation may not be as satisfied as this generation is.

High and low

"I don't get as excited as I used to get, but I do feel more content." That's how a sixty-year-old explained her emotions.

We seem to move on a more even keel. The newest fads and trends may not set us off, but disappointment doesn't drag us down as far either. We've seen more of life. We've survived its great joys as well as its heartaches. We tend to be more stable, less flaky, and more dependable.

When a television ad claims to offer the "immortal songs" of some singer, we know better. If a local furniture store advertises a "once in a lifetime offer," we no longer bolt out of our chairs and hustle across town. Politicians who say they will lower taxes and increase benefits don't give us goose pimples anymore.

Not that we have become cynical. But we aren't so easily excited about amazing offers or outlandish claims. We know Elvis is dead and we don't look for him at the local convenience store.

Even-handed. Calm. Cool. Steady. Faithful.

The only real security.

While we look for financial security, millions at our age know there is only one source of real security. Pensions fall apart. Houses blow away. People die. Markets drop. Even governments fail and crumble. Only God offers us total security for eternity.

Our faith in God becomes the anchor for our souls. God is the anchor which will not be moved.

"We have this hope as an anchor for the soul, firm and secure" (Hebrews 6:19).

The book of Job shows a great understanding of the problem. If our trust is fixed solely on wealth, we have turned away from God and have become unfaithful to Him.

Read Job 31:24–28. The passage is strong and colorful. For our purpose let us quote only the first and last verses.

"If I have put my trust in gold or said to pure gold, 'You are my security,' . . . I would have been unfaithful to God on high" (Job 31:24 and 28).

Regularly we read about homes that collapse into sink holes and everything is lost. Floods have engulfed farms. Someone recently built a beautiful home on the edge of a cliff in California. When the mudslides came, the house slipped down the side of the mountain. No one remembers exactly when they realized that the home was uninsured.

All of us need to aim for security, but we also must remember that security outside of Christ is mostly an illusion.

The author of Proverbs draws a vivid picture of the Lord as a fortress. Within that fort there is not only a safe place for each of us as parents but also it can serve to protect our children.

Those of us who depend on that fort, the one where the walls cannot be destroyed, point the way for our children. Hopefully they will find security in the same place where we find it.

"He who fears the LORD has a secure fortress, and for his children it will be a refuge" (Proverbs 14:26).

Not the children of gloom

The author of Ecclesiastes has an attitude. Even a casual reading of the book shows him to be a real pessimist. Life is empty; as he sees it, nothing is going to work out. They are dead flies in the perfume, everything is chasing the wind.

But, despite his dour outlook on life, the author gives us this great advice: Make every year the best year of your life.

"However many years a man may live, let him enjoy them all" (Ecclesiastes 11:8).

Tomorrow could be tough. None of us knows what unexpected events wait for us. Today needs to be fulfilling, satisfying, giving, loving, sacrificing. There is no way to know what tomorrow might offer (Matthew 6:34).

These can be the best years of our lives. Not the most selfish or self-centered but the most enjoyable. For those who claim them, they are often exactly that.

Note to the Reader

The publisher invites you to share your response to the message of this book by writing Discovery House Publishers, P. O. Box 3566, Grand Rapids, MI 49501, U.S.A. or by calling 1-800-653-8333. For information about other Discovery House publications, contact us at the same address and phone number.